Telephone Continuing Care Therapy for Adults

Telephone Continuing Care Therapy for Adults

James R. McKay, Ph.D.
Deborah H. A. Van Horn, Ph.D.
Rebecca Morrison, R.N., M.A.

HAZELDEN®

Hazelden
Center City, Minnesota 55012
hazelden.org

© 2010 by James R. McKay, Deborah H. A. Van Horn, and Rebecca Morrison
All rights reserved. Published 2010
Printed in the United States of America

The workbook and forms on the CD-ROM may be duplicated for personal or group use. Otherwise, no part of this publication may be reproduced, stored in a retrieval system, or transmitted in any form or by any means—electronic, mechanical, photocopying, recording, scanning, or otherwise—without the express written permission of the publisher. Failure to comply with these terms may expose you to legal action and damages for copyright infringement.

ISBN: 978-1-59285-745-6

Editor's note
The names, details, and circumstances may have been changed to protect the privacy of those mentioned in this publication.

This publication is not intended as a substitute for the advice of health care professionals.

Alcoholics Anonymous and AA are registered trademarks of Alcoholics Anonymous World Services, Inc.

J. R. McKay, K. G. Lynch, D. S. Shepard, S. Ratichek, R. Morrison, J. Koppenhaver, and H. M. Pettinati, "The Effectiveness of Telephone-Based Continuing Care in the Clinical Management of Alcohol and Cocaine Use Disorders: 12-Month Outcomes," *Journal of Consulting and Clinical Psychology* 72, no. 6 (2004): 967–79, copyright © 2004 by the American Psychological Association, has been included on the CD-ROM with permission. No further reproduction or distribution is permitted without written permission from the American Psychological Association. The use of this information does not imply endorsement by the publisher.

The abstract of J. R. McKay, K. G. Lynch, D. S. Shepard, and H. M. Pettinati, "The Effectiveness of Telephone-Based Continuing Care for Alcohol and Cocaine Dependence: 24-Month Outcomes," *Archives of General Psychiatry* 62 (2005): 199–207, copyright © 2005 American Medical Association, all rights reserved, has been included on the CD-ROM with permission. No further reproduction or distribution is permitted without written permission from the American Medical Association. The use of this information does not imply endorsement by the publisher.

Cover and interior design by David Farr, ImageSmythe
Typesetting by David Farr, ImageSmythe

Hazelden, a national nonprofit organization founded in 1949, helps people reclaim their lives from the disease of addiction. Built on decades of knowledge and experience, Hazelden offers a comprehensive approach to addiction that addresses the full range of patient, family, and professional needs, including treatment and continuing care for youth and adults, research, higher learning, public education and advocacy, and publishing.

A life of recovery is lived "one day at a time." Hazelden publications, both educational and inspirational, support and strengthen lifelong recovery. In 1954, Hazelden published *Twenty-Four Hours a Day*, the first daily meditation book for recovering alcoholics, and Hazelden continues to publish works to inspire and guide individuals in treatment and recovery, and their loved ones. Professionals who work to prevent and treat addiction also turn to Hazelden for evidence-based curricula, informational materials, and videos for use in schools, treatment programs, and correctional programs.

Through published works, Hazelden extends the reach of hope, encouragement, help, and support to individuals, families, and communities affected by addiction and related issues.

For questions about Hazelden publications, please call **800-328-9000** or visit us online at **hazelden.org/bookstore.**

Contents

Acknowledgments vii

Introduction 1

Chapter 1 Understanding the Program 5
Chapter 2 Therapy Models 13
Chapter 3 The Therapeutic Alliance 23
Chapter 4 The Orientation Session 29
Chapter 5 The Telephone-Based Sessions 41
Chapter 6 Adaptive Algorithms for Stepped Care 55
Chapter 7 Maximizing Adherence
 to Telephone Continuing Care 67

References 75
About the Authors 79

Acknowledgments

WE ARE DEEPLY GRATEFUL to the counselors who have contributed to the development and evaluation of the telephone continuing care protocol that is described in this manual: Oubah Abdalla, Sarah Domis, Angela Hackman, Daniel Herd, Dara Herskovits, and Tyrone Thomas. Their input, feedback, and clinical discussions about patients in our studies were essential factors in the successful evolution of the intervention. We have also very much appreciated our ongoing collaborations with several publicly funded programs in the Philadelphia area, which served as sites for our continuing care research projects, and the consistent support of the Philadelphia Department of Behavioral Health. In addition, we thank the Philadelphia Veterans Affairs Medical Center, which has also been a partner in this work. None of this work would have been possible without the participation of more than two thousand patients, who generously provided their time over periods as long as twenty-four months and who remained committed to our studies, even when they were randomized to treatment conditions that were not their first choice. Finally, we thank the National Institute on Alcohol Abuse and Alcoholism and the National Institute on Drug Abuse for providing the funding for the four studies in which this intervention was developed and evaluated.

Introduction

A GROWING INTEREST IN NEW MODELS OF TREATMENT is bringing the addictions field into a new era. These treatment protocols and systems address the full continuum of care, from detoxification to extended recovery monitoring (ASAM 2001; Dennis and Scott 2007; Dennis, Scott, and Funk 2003; Humphreys and Tucker 2002; McKay 2005; McLellan et al. 2000; Simpson 2004). In this new era, care will be provided in contemporary client-centered models designed to effectively manage chronic disorders (IOM 2006; Wagner et al. 2001).

Several factors are driving these changes, including progressive state and local leadership, more open-mindedness and pragmatism among treatment providers, increasing insistence from all stakeholders for better outcomes, and influential publications that have pointed out the similarities between addiction and other chronic disorders and the limitations of the current addiction treatment system (McLellan et al. 2000; McLellan, Carise, and Kleber 2003). In addition, research literature on continuing care has provided important information on the effectiveness of various interventions and management practices, ranging from more traditional Twelve Step–focused group counseling approaches to flexible extended care models (Dennis and Scott 2007; McKay 2005; McKay 2009a; McKay 2009b).

The term *continuing care* has been used to indicate the stage of treatment that follows an initial episode of more intensive care, usually inpatient/residential or intensive outpatient treatment. At one point, this phase of care was referred to as *aftercare*, but the more common term is now *continuing care*, which better conveys the idea that active treatment continues in this phase (McKay 2005). Continuing care is provided in a variety of formats and modalities, including group counseling, individual therapy, telephone counseling, brief checkups, and peer-support meetings. This manual presents an approach to continuing care that relies primarily on telephone contacts.

A User-Friendly Intervention

Although there is now widespread agreement among clinicians, policy makers, and treatment researchers that continuing care is important, it is not always easy to deliver. Availability is a major problem. Some programs have provided little or no formal continuing care because insurance reimbursement has been limited. However, lack of availability is not the whole story. Some clients will not participate in continuing care when it *is* available and covered by insurance because they do not want to keep coming back to the clinic for further treatment sessions. This reluctance can reflect diminished motivation for treatment, but it can also be the result of other competing factors, such as the need to attend to work and parenting responsibilities.

This suggests that there is a need for a flexible, user-friendly continuing care intervention that can be provided for extended periods, if necessary. The challenge is to develop an effective intervention that is more appealing and less burdensome to clients than standard continuing care in order to promote higher participation rates. One possibility is to center the intervention on the use of regular, relatively brief telephone contacts, with provisions to "step up" the level of care when a client's status or symptoms indicate increased risk of relapse (Lavori, Dawson, and Rush 2000; McKay 2009a; Sobell and Sobell 2000).

Telephone-based continuing care is appealing to clients for a number of reasons. First, it is more convenient than standard, clinic-based care. Clients do not have to have access to transportation, take time off from work, or arrange for child care in order to travel to the clinic. Calls can be completed from home, work, or other locations where the client might be at the scheduled time of the session. Second, telephone-based interventions are provided via individual sessions. Conversely, most standard continuing care is provided in groups, a modality that many clients do not like. Third, this approach provides support outside of conventional chemical-dependency treatment programs. Some clients are concerned about the perceived stigma associated with participation in such programs and wish to receive continuing care in some other setting.

A Useful Treatment Component

With regard to effectiveness, the telephone is considered to have a viable therapeutic role in the treatment of a number of physical and mental health problems (Roter et al. 1998; Wasson et al. 1992). Various studies have supported its use in the delivery of reactive and proactive counseling interventions, and in the therapeutic monitoring of health status, treatment compliance, and risk behavior. Telephone contact has been a useful component in the monitoring and treatment of depression (Baer et al. 1995; Osgood-Hynes et al. 1998) and obsessive-compulsive disorder (Baer et al. 1993; Greist et al. 1998).

Telephone counseling has been used most extensively as a component in smoking cessation programs. A meta-analysis has shown proactive calls made by clinicians to study clients have consistently produced better smoking outcomes than control conditions (Lichtenstein et al. 1996). There have been fewer studies of telephone continuing care in the treatment of alcohol and other drug disorders. In a study with problem drinkers, Connors, Tarbox, and Faillace (1992) reported no differences between group counseling, telephone calls, and a no-continuing-care control condition on drinking outcome measures, although the sample size in this study was small. Conversely, Foote and Erfurt (1991) reported that extended telephone contacts in an employee assistance program (EAP) produced better outcomes than standard follow-up care, as indicated by fewer subsequent hospitalizations and lower substance abuse treatment costs. More recently, Horng and Chueh (2004) reported that a three-month telephone continuing care intervention produced better alcohol use outcomes than a no-continuing-care comparison condition.

The telephone-based continuing care protocol presented in this manual was developed over the course of four randomized clinical trials conducted at the University of Pennsylvania. These studies are described in more detail later in the manual.

This manual consists of a detailed description of the program and outlines for the face-to-face orientation session and the subsequent telephone-based sessions. There are also guidelines for administering the stepped-care component and maximizing adherence to the treatment protocols. The CD-ROM that accompanies the manual contains a client workbook, client handouts, forms for documenting treatment progress, and relevant journal articles.

Chapter 1

Understanding the Program

THIS PROGRAM IS DESIGNED TO PROVIDE continuing care for clients who have completed a residential treatment program or an intensive outpatient program for a substance use disorder. The majority of the sessions are provided via telephone contacts. However, we have found that some clients prefer to come into the clinic for some of their sessions. The program also includes a stepped-care component, which can include a return to clinic-based care, at least for brief periods of time. Therefore, some sessions will likely be provided in the clinic or office.

The sessions are usually offered on a weekly basis for eight weeks, twice monthly for another ten months, and, if desired, monthly after that for up to a total of two years. Each session is fifteen to thirty minutes in length and begins with a brief structured Progress Assessment of current symptoms and functioning. This assessment generates summary scores for relapse risk and protective factors, which can be used to monitor changes in these areas over time and to structure the rest of the session. These scores also provide guidance on possible increases or decreases in treatment intensity (that is, stepped care). The rest of the session is then focused on developing coping responses to risk factors identified in the assessment or expected over the period before the next session, primarily through the use of techniques from cognitive-behavioral therapy (CBT). Motivational interviewing (MI) techniques are also used, particularly when the client appears to be losing motivation or becomes less involved with pro-recovery activities.

The stepped-care component has been included to adapt the program to the changing needs of the client over time. When a client's balance of risk and protective factors shifts sufficiently in the wrong direction, more frequent telephone calls are first offered. If this does not provide enough support and structure, an in-person evaluation session based on MI principles is recommended, to be followed by a course of face-to-face CBT sessions if the evaluation session finds that level of support is needed. Each component of the program is described in detail later in this manual.

Which Treatment Settings Can Use This Program?

This program can be used in a wide range of treatment settings and facilities. Residential or inpatient programs can use it to provide continuing care to clients after they leave the facility. In rural areas, where clients may travel some distance to attend either residential or outpatient treatment, the program can be used to provide continuing care following completion of a more intensive level of care, whether inpatient or outpatient. In such situations, the program may be limited primarily to telephone contact, with less opportunity for face-to-face stepped-care sessions.

The program can also be used by outpatient facilities to provide ongoing recovery support during and after intensive outpatient or standard outpatient treatment. For example, an intensive outpatient program (IOP) could start clients on the telephone program in their last month of IOP and continue it for some period of time after discharge. It is also possible to start the program earlier in the treatment process for higher-risk clients in order to provide additional individualized support and prevent early dropout. In our current research projects, for example, we begin providing the program to IOP clients in their third week of treatment. The city of Philadelphia recently began a pilot program with uninsured clients seeking treatment in the publicly funded system. This telephone recovery support protocol was provided at the very beginning of treatment, to prevent high-risk clients from falling through the cracks in the system.

How Is This Program Different from Other Outpatient/Continuing Care Programs?

An obvious difference is that this program is provided primarily via telephone contact, rather than face-to-face sessions. However, there are a number of other differences:

- The program is designed for one-to-one sessions rather than a group format.
- Each session begins with a structured Progress Assessment of risk and protective factors.
- The focus of the work in each session is guided by the assessment results.
- There is an emphasis on working on specific coping responses to risky situations.
- Progress on decreasing risk and increasing protective factors is monitored and tracked over time.
- Specific guidelines are provided for when and how to change level of care, based on changes in risk and protective factors over time.

Are Extra Staff Members Needed to Manage the Program?

Several factors determine whether additional staff members are needed to implement this program. Most clinicians have some time during the day when they would be available to deliver the telephone protocol. Given that each session is typically fifteen to twenty minutes long (although they can be up to thirty minutes long), a clinician could do three sessions in an hour, provided that clients were available at that time. Therefore, a program might be able to provide up to three months of telephone contact (that is, ten calls) to program graduates without needing much additional staffing. Often, clinicians who are providing IOP or residential care find it rewarding to be able to follow their graduates after they have completed an initial phase of treatment.

On the other hand, additional staff will clearly be needed if a treatment facility decides to implement the program earlier in the treatment process or to extend it over longer periods of time. For example, the potential pool of program recipients is much larger if it is provided to all clients in an IOP, as opposed to only those clients who complete that phase of care. In addition, the stepped-care component of the program, which includes individual CBT sessions, can require additional staffing. However, it should be stressed that the version of the program that was evaluated and found to be effective in our first two studies did not include a stepped-care component. Therefore, treatment facilities could opt to try to reengage clients back into their standard programming should stepped care be required, rather than provide the individual CBT described here.

Finally, we have found that computerizing some aspects of the program, particularly the recording and tracking of risk and protective factor scores from the Progress Assessment at the start of each session, can be helpful to clinicians delivering the program. These data can be collected via paper and pencil, but it is more difficult to quickly review changes over time in the absence of a database. At this point, software that performs these functions is not available. Therefore, some staff time may be needed to set up a database if the facility desires to computerize the data collection process.

What Special Issues Might Arise When Dealing with Different Cultural Groups?

The majority of clients who have participated in our studies of telephone continuing care have been African Americans. We have looked at whether there are any differences in outcomes between African American and white clients, or between men and women, and have found no evidence that such differences are present (Lynch et al. 2009; McKay et al. 2003).

What about Clients with Co-occurring Disorders?

Clients who were currently exhibiting psychotic symptoms of sufficient strength to interfere with treatment have not participated in our studies of telephone continuing care, nor have clients with severe cognitive deficits. Therefore, it is not clear whether the intervention would be effective with such clients. However, we have included clients with other co-occurring psychiatric disorders in our studies, including schizophrenia-spectrum disorders, major depression, bipolar disorder, and anxiety disorders, including post-traumatic stress disorder (PTSD). Analyses indicate that neither a history of major depression nor current severity of psychiatric symptoms at the beginning of the program predicts poorer substance use outcomes in telephone continuing care as compared to face-to-face interventions (McKay et al. 2005a). It should be noted that we have required clients with major psychiatric disorders, such as major depression or bipolar disorder, to have met with a psychiatrist and have been evaluated for medication in order to be in our studies. Some follow-up with a psychiatrist is also recommended for such clients.

Clients with a range of other co-occurring problems, such as poverty, poor social support, medical disorders, and criminal justice involvement, have participated in our studies. Procedures for addressing co-occurring problems are presented later in this manual. The Progress Assessment that is done at the beginning of each call includes information on factors such as psychiatric symptoms, work, and social support in order to monitor these areas and guide interventions.

Is the Program Evidence Based?

This program has been evaluated in four randomized research studies, all of which have provided evidence of its effectiveness. These studies have featured large sample sizes, two-year follow-ups, high follow-up rates, and confirmation of self-reported alcohol and drug use outcomes with biological tests or collateral reports. The studies were all conducted in publicly funded clinics in Philadelphia or in a Veterans Affairs Medical Center program, with clients who had extensive histories of alcohol and cocaine use, multiple prior treatment episodes, and high rates of co-occurring problems such as poverty, psychiatric disorders, and lack of social support for recovery.

The initial two studies (available on the CD-ROM) were conducted with clients who had completed four-week IOPs. A twelve-week version of the telephone-based continuing care intervention was found to be more effective than "treatment as usual" continuing care in the clinic (twelve weeks of group counseling) on most alcohol and drug use outcome measures. The intervention was also more effective than twelve weeks of cognitive-behavioral relapse prevention continuing care on some outcomes (McKay et al. 2004; McKay et al. 2005b). In the third study, we extended the intervention out to eighteen months and tested it in clients who had completed at least three weeks of more extended IOP. Once again, the intervention produced better alcohol and drug use outcomes than the comparison conditions—in this case, IOP without telephone continuing care, and IOP with telephone calls that provided monitoring and very brief feedback but no counseling (McKay et al. 2009a; McKay 2009a). In the fourth study, which is currently under way, we are looking at the impact of providing small incentives for completing the telephone continuing care contacts.

The first two studies are completed and have been published in professional journals. The third study is completed, and data out to the eighteen-month follow-up for the complete sample have been presented at professional conferences. Two papers from this study are currently under review (Lynch et al. 2009; McKay et al. 2009b). The fourth study is still in process, although preliminary data out to the nine-month follow-up are positive as well.

How Should Clients Be Identified and Selected for Participation?

The telephone continuing care protocol can be offered to two groups:

- graduates of an initial, more intensive phase of care, such as residential treatment or IOP treatment
- clients who are still in OP or IOP treatment, but who may be at risk for dropout

If the goal is to offer the program to graduates of an initial phase of treatment, clients in residential or IOP treatment should be approached in the last week or two of treatment and told about the availability of the telephone continuing care program. It should be described as one of several options for continuing care, which also may include clinic-based care and/or peer-support programs. These options are not mutually exclusive; for example, clients could participate in the telephone program and attend AA or even group counseling. The important considerations are whether the client is motivated to participate in some form of continuing care and whether the telephone program is particularly appealing. Clients who anticipate difficulties attending standard clinic-based continuing care due to transportation problems, parental or work responsibilities, or a desire to "move on" with their recovery may be particularly good candidates for telephone-based continuing care.

If the goal of offering telephone continuing care is to provide additional recovery support to clients while they are attending an IOP, clients can be considered immediately for the program. In our studies, we have waited until clients have been in an IOP for at least two weeks before enrolling them in the research project. Therefore, it is not clear how effective the program is for clients who have not been in treatment that long. Although we would expect higher dropout rates among clients who are offered the program at or shortly after intake, there are likely to be some at-risk clients in this group who would benefit from the support provided by telephone contact.

If possible, we recommend that clients begin this protocol prior to graduating from their initial treatment program in order to increase the likelihood that they will make a successful transition to continuing care. Initial levels of care range considerably in duration; for example, some IOPs are only two weeks long, whereas others are three or four months in duration. Given the high rate of dropout in most outpatient programs, it is important to engage the client in the telephone protocol before he or she either graduates or drops out of the initial phase of care. During the period of overlap, when the client is still attending an IOP or OP and having telephone sessions, the calls place a greater emphasis on supporting continued engagement in that program. This is done by addressing barriers to attendance, such as problems with transportation, family roles, or employment; diminishing motivation for treatment or recovery; or problems with the IOP or OP itself.

Another important consideration in the selection of clients for the telephone program is what other continuing care options are available to the client. Our research indicates that some high-risk clients will do better if they receive twice-weekly clinic-based group counseling rather than telephone continuing care (McKay et al. 2005a). In this study, "high risk" was determined by failure to progress toward the main goals of the IOP along with whether the client was dependent on more than one substance at entrance to the IOP. The IOP goals, assessed over the past thirty days at the end of the IOP, were as follows:

- abstinence from cocaine
- abstinence from alcohol
- commitment to total abstinence
- attendance at three or more self-help group meetings per week

- at least 80-percent confidence in being able to use coping behaviors to avoid relapse
- some degree of social support for abstinence

Also added to this index was dependence on both alcohol and cocaine upon entrance to treatment. Clients who had *any combination* of four or more of these seven factors (that is, dependence on both alcohol and cocaine and failure to achieve three IOP goals, dependence on alcohol only but failure to achieve four IOP goals, and so on) did better in twice-weekly group counseling than in telephone continuing care. This effect was present through month twenty-one of the twenty-four-month follow-up. In our sample, only 20 percent of the clients were categorized in this high-risk group, quite probably because the sample was limited to those who completed a four-week IOP.

If clients have the option of participating in structured continuing care at the clinic after the IOP has ended, it makes sense to consider their progress in an IOP before recommending telephone continuing care. Clients who have done poorly in an IOP may be better served by remaining at that level of care for a few more weeks in order to achieve more of the goals listed here or starting off in clinic-based continuing care rather than moving directly to telephone continuing care only.

Chapter 2

Therapy Models

OUR TELEPHONE CONTINUING CARE MODEL is based on the principles of cognitive-behavioral therapy (CBT). According to the theories on which CBT is based, substance use is viewed as a learned habit that occurs in the context of environmental triggers, intra-individual thoughts and feelings, and short- and long-term consequences. Treatment involves identifying the client's unique triggers for substance use so that he or she can learn to avoid them or cope more effectively with them, and helping the client learn and practice more adaptive coping skills for managing risky situations (Carroll 1998).

It is important to emphasize that clinicians do not have to believe that addiction is a learned habit in order to use this program. Whatever the etiology of substance use disorders may be—learned habit, brain disease, self-medication, purely environmental, or some combination of any of these factors—clients can benefit by receiving help in monitoring their progress and developing improved coping behaviors for the stressful or high-risk situations they encounter in their daily lives. The program has been used successfully with clients who embrace the Alcoholics Anonymous view of the origins of substance use disorders and with clients who attribute their addiction to environmental factors such as family or the neighborhood they come from.

Intervention in CBT is based on a careful functional analysis of the client's alcohol and drug use. Substance use is viewed as a learned behavior that is associated with certain environmental antecedents and consequences, and placing the client's substance use in its individual context guides selection of interventions.

1. **Environmental antecedents to drinking/drug use**—the external and interpersonal situations in which substance use is most likely. Clients need to learn to recognize high-risk situations and either avoid them or learn to cope with them without picking up. In telephone continuing care, clients monitor the risky situations they encounter and learn to anticipate upcoming risky situations in the intervals between phone calls. Over time, clients are encouraged to make lifestyle choices that limit their exposure to risky situations.

2. **Thoughts, feelings, and cravings**—the link between external high-risk situations and the client's behavioral response. The client thinks that a drink would taste good, have a pleasant effect, or improve an unpleasant mood or problematic situation, so he starts drinking. Or the client feels confident in her ability to wait out an unpleasant mood, so she focuses on the benefits of abstinence and engages in an alternative activity. Nearly all clients experience urges or cravings, especially in early abstinence, that often seem to come out of the blue. It is essential for them to develop a repertoire of coping skills to fall back on when cravings arise. Some situations may be so closely associated with substance use that they elicit cravings or even relapses seemingly without any thoughts on the client's part, but over time most clients learn to identify and challenge their thoughts and beliefs about substance use.

3. **Behavior**—substance use or abstinence in response to an environmental trigger or craving. Simply "not drinking" or "not using" doesn't describe behavior, so when planning for high-risk situations or reviewing a "close call," the clinician needs to help the client identify alternative actions. At the level of a specific incident, if the client encountered a high-risk situation and didn't drink, what did he do instead? At a lifestyle level, clients need to develop a range of enjoyable activities that are inconsistent with alcohol and drug use.

4. **Consequences**—the results of either drinking or doing something else. Usually the short-term consequences of

drinking and drug use are positive, for example, feeling euphoric, socializing, taking a break from the work of recovery, or forgetting one's problems. It is often the longer-term consequences that are the problem. For pro-recovery behavior, the situation is usually the reverse, with the short-term consequences ranging from enjoyment of a sober activity (which may pale in comparison to an alcohol or drug high) to the genuine displeasure of dealing with life's misfortunes. The true benefits of sobriety may take much longer to realize. The phone sessions will provide an opportunity for the client to recall the negative consequences of drinking and to review the benefits of maintaining sobriety and completing personal goals.

Many substance abusers view themselves as people that things "happen" to—things over which they have little or no control. One goal of cognitive-behavioral relapse prevention counseling is to help clients become more aware of the connections between their behavior and what happens to them. The clinician may need to help a client recognize these connections. From our experience, this is more difficult to do over the phone than in person. So the clinician may need to prompt the client more often to be specific about the chain of events, and his or her role in setting the events in motion, while delivering telephone continuing care. A second goal is to help the client get into the habit of anticipating upcoming risky situations in order to cope with them more proactively. Consistent use of the "behavior chain"—linking situations, thoughts/feelings, behavior, and results—will help clients to describe their behavior in a manner amenable to problem solving.

The key components of CBT that are used in this program really boil down to the following four elements:

- Develop an understanding of what factors led to relapses in the past.
- Learn to anticipate such high-risk situations.
- Identify or develop better coping responses to these situations.
- Practice these new coping responses both during the call and in the period before the next call.

In addition, the protocol places a heavy emphasis on weekly goals that are agreed upon by the clinician and client and are carefully monitored during the course of the treatment.

The Clinician's Role in Telephone-Based Continuing Care

CBT is a collaborative approach in which the clinician and client work together toward agreed-upon goals. In face-to-face CBT as a primary treatment for addiction, the clinician's role is often didactic, instructing the client about the nature of her problem and teaching new skills to overcome substance abuse. In telephone continuing care, the clinician is less didactic and functions more as a coach, guiding the client to use what she has learned in—and out of—treatment to progress toward her goals.

Increasingly, attention has been paid in CBT to strengthening motivation and commitment to change. Recent manuals have incorporated motivational interviewing (MI) techniques into CBT, often as an initial step prior to beginning skills training (Miller 2004). Similarly, we encourage use of selected MI techniques as part of the process of developing rapport and encouraging engagement at the start of treatment. Throughout treatment, we find that using an MI-consistent communication style complements the CBT content of the program and is also consistent with the less didactic "coaching" role of the clinician in telephone continuing care. The clinician remains active and provides structure, but the client is encouraged to be proactive and resourceful, rather than relying on the clinician's instructions. Furthermore, use of MI style helps the clinician to attend to fluctuating motivation over time and address it as it occurs. Often, simply "rolling with" resistance as it occurs is all that is needed, but when motivation is flagging, it is relatively straightforward for the clinician to switch away from coaching coping skills to exploring motivation for change.

More about MI in Continuing Care

Motivational interviewing has been defined as "a client-centered, directive method for increasing intrinsic motivation by exploring and resolving ambivalence" (Miller and Rollnick 2002). In MI, the clinician uses a client-centered counseling style strategically to elicit "change talk" and minimize resistance. The client-centered style is common to many forms of counseling and is familiar to CBT practitioners as a means to establish rapport and help get the client "on board" with treatment.

The client-centered counseling style in which MI is delivered is characterized by four "microskills." This is captured by the acronym OARS, which refers to open-ended questions, affirming, reflective listening, and summarizing.

The first microskill is asking *open-ended questions*. Open-ended questions tend to elicit broad, informative, reflective answers. They are useful for getting more information about where the client is in relation to readiness to change without appearing to be judgmental or leading the client. Open-ended questions are preferable to closed questions during all stages of the process. Most of the techniques associated with eliciting change talk rely on asking good open questions.

The second microskill is *affirming*. It is a way of validating the client's experiences and feelings. Validation is not something frequently experienced by most drug and alcohol abusers since their concerns are often ignored or written off as lies or manipulations by significant others and service providers. Affirmations can focus on the client's strengths or on the client's efforts toward change. Many clients can learn how to self-affirm when thoughts or feelings are accepted by significant others. These supportive comments encourage clients to believe in themselves and resolve ambivalence by marshaling their resources to take positive action and change behavior. Examples of affirmative responses are "That must have been very hard for you" or "You have already come a long way toward solving this problem." Affirmations are particularly useful to help reduce the hopelessness, discouragement, and isolation that clients may feel when struggling with maintaining a sober lifestyle or regaining sobriety after a relapse.

The third microskill is *reflective listening*. This skill can be used in a client-centered manner to demonstrate that the clinician has accurately heard and understood what the client is saying and used in a directive manner to strengthen motivational themes. So-called simple reflections stay close to the client's stated meaning by repeating or rephrasing the client's words. Complex reflections use paraphrasing, continuing the paragraph, metaphor, and reflection of feeling to guess at the client's underlying meaning (Miller et al. 2003). Both have their uses in MI, with simple reflections allowing the client to feel heard and understood, and complex reflections serving to deepen the relationship and move the session in a different direction. In most cases, reflective listening invites further elaboration: the client can confirm or reject the restatement and then continue to elaborate on the subject, if so inclined.

The fourth and last microskill is *summarizing* what the client has said during an interview or even a part of an interview. It is an opportunity for the clinician to strategically select information that should be included and minimize or leave out other information. This technique allows a client to consider the clinician's responses and then contemplate his own experiences. Summarizing is a good way to reflect back to the client his ambivalence. It can also be used to simply state several thoughts that the client has expressed and invite the client to continue to elaborate. For example, the clinician might say, after summarizing, "So where do you go from here?" or "What are your thoughts about all of this?" or "Did I leave anything out?"

Change Talk

Change talk may be defined as client speech that indicates movement toward greater readiness for change. The clinician's task during MI is to elicit change talk from the client, rather than be the one making the argument for change. The directive aspect of MI involves eliciting, reflecting, and amplifying change talk, while also minimizing resistance.

Change talk may be categorized as follows (Amrhein et al. 2003):

- desire for change
- ability for change
- reasons for change
- need for change
- commitment for change

Of these categories, the first four may be viewed as "preparatory" language that is associated with an increase in commitment for change. Commitment language, particularly toward the end of a session, is associated with better behavior change outcomes.

The typical manner of eliciting change talk in MI, and particularly when combining MI and CBT, is to ask open-ended questions that focus the client's attention on behavior change and responding in a manner that heightens the client's perceived importance of and confidence for change.

Clients who are ambivalent about change, or whose motivation to maintain change is diminishing, will make statements often viewed as evidence of "denial" of a problem. Rather than confronting denial or resistance head-on, the clinician using MI will "roll with" resistance, usually through skillful use of reflective listening. The clinician uses reflective listening to convey understanding of the client's perspective and avoids getting into an unproductive argument in which the client continually defends her reasons to remain out of treatment while the clinician argues for reengagement. MI may be considered a "constructive discussion about behavior change" (Rollnick, Mason, and Butler 1999), and the aim of these techniques is to return to a constructive discussion as quickly as possible.

As stated above, the main method for managing resistance in MI is to use reflective listening. Simple reflections, staying close to the client's stated content and level of readiness for change, generally convey an understanding of the client's concerns and can serve to defuse resistance.

Amplified reflections, in which the client's resistance is reflected back in a somewhat exaggerated manner, often elicit a backpedaling response away from the resistant statement. Double-sided reflections, including both change talk and resistance, encourage working through ambivalence.

> *Client:* **I got three years of sobriety by going to meetings, but this time around I just can't get into it. It's the same thing, over and over again.**
>
> *Clinician (simple reflection):* **You're having a hard time getting motivated to go to meetings.**
>
> *Clinician (amplified reflection):* **You think meetings are useless.**
>
> *Clinician (double-sided reflection):* **Something's getting in the way of going to meetings, even though you know they can be helpful to you.**

Resistance may also be managed on a strategic level, for example, by emphasizing the resistant client's control over whether and how to change, reframing the client's resistant statements into opportunities to explore options for change, or guiding the conversation away from what the client won't do to what he is willing to consider.

> *Client:* **I got three years of sobriety by going to meetings, but this time around I just can't get into it. It's the same thing, over and over again.**
>
> *Clinician (reframing):* **You want to feel excited about recovery again, and you haven't found the right support group yet.**

In our model of CBT-based continuing care, MI style is used primarily to increase client motivation for and engagement in ongoing monitoring, problem solving, and enacting chosen solutions to anticipated problems. Therefore, there is considerably more activity and direction on the part of the clinician than in a purely MI-based intervention. The clinician is informed by the insights of the MI approach to remain alert to fluctuations in motivation and to be prepared to address decreases in motivation appropriately.

"Regular" CBT versus Telephone-Based Continuing Care

CBT in telephone continuing care maintains the same basic principles as CBT as a primary treatment, with some important differences in practice. Rather than teach a core set of skills for recovery, we help the client to engage in week-to-week management of her addiction. Therefore, the agenda of each session is not tied to the client's completion of tasks related to each topic or skill, but rather to ongoing assessment of the client's substance use, relapse risk, and progress toward developing a rewarding, substance-free lifestyle. Certainly, learning to self-monitor relapse risk and pro-recovery lifestyle behavior may be seen as an essential skill for maintaining abstinence, but for the most part, we de-emphasize teaching coping skills in favor of identifying and reinforcing use of existing skills. This approach is more feasible in relatively brief telephone calls.

Telephone continuing care was developed to follow completion of an IOP and is conceptualized in terms of maintaining and building upon treatment gains regardless of whether the client has achieved initial abstinence. Consistent with cognitive-behavioral relapse prevention, we focus not only on eliminating substance use but also on building a balanced lifestyle rich in intrinsically rewarding activities. We provide a basic orientation to treatment, but we also assume that clients have been exposed to certain key concepts, regardless of the orientation of the IOP. For example, we assume that clients have been introduced to the idea that being in certain situations is more likely to result in substance use and that they have begun to identify those situations. Therefore, our assessment of the client's substance use history is much briefer than it would be in CBT as a primary treatment. We conceptualize use in terms of functional assessment but do not spend time building up the client's patterns of use from detailed analysis of specific episodes. Rather, we begin with clients' self-report of their environmental triggers for use. However, we process relapses in terms of functional analysis, and, similarly, we model and guide clients through problem solving rather than explicitly teach them how to solve their problems.

Attention is paid to cognitive factors in achieving and maintaining abstinence, but the focus to a greater degree is on use of behavioral coping skills. Cognitive coping skills, such as thinking through the drink or reminding oneself of the rewards of sobriety, are emphasized over extensive challenging of negative automatic thoughts. The emphasis on behavioral coping is practical: Calls are brief, Socratic questioning is more difficult over the phone than in person, and there is little opportunity in routine monitoring and counseling to teach the client to challenge dysfunctional thoughts in a formal way.

Our model of telephone continuing care was developed pragmatically and therefore includes some elements that are not typical of CBT as a primary treatment. One area is our choice of elements to include in the Progress Assessment conducted at each contact. In addition to items characteristic of CBT, such as coping with high-risk situations, we have included items reflecting factors associated in prior research with outcome, so that they can be addressed as needed. One such factor is depression. Based on prior research showing poorer outcome among clients with current depression, we screen for persistent depressed mood at each contact and are quick to make referrals to additional treatment. Another such factor is Twelve Step meeting attendance. We do not insist on meeting attendance, nor do we spend a lot of time exploring barriers to attendance among clients who are firmly opposed to participating, but we do inform clients that we have found that those who attend more Twelve Step meetings tend to do better over time, and that we will therefore monitor their attendance and active participation among other "protective" factors such as use of proactive coping and development of rewarding sober activities.

Another area in which our practice diverges from more traditional CBT practice is in our use of Twelve Step and "recovery" language when presenting concepts and engaging the client in problem solving. We are aware that most of our clients enter telephone continuing care having been in Twelve Step–oriented treatment programs, and therefore are more likely to be familiar with terms like "people, places, and things" than with the phrase "environmental antecedents." We often refer to periods of sustained abstinence and improved psychosocial functioning as "recovery." Rather than attempt to teach a new set of terminology, we use familiar phrases when possible. Similarly, while we do not explicitly espouse a disease model, so many aspects of managing a chronic disease are essentially the same as those involved in modifying a learned behavior that we do not spend time challenging a disease model and explicitly substituting a learned-behavior model.

Chapter 3

The Therapeutic Alliance

TELEPHONE-BASED CONTINUING CARE is less burdensome to clients, and most report that they like this form of treatment delivery. However, it can also be more difficult for clinicians to deliver, because of the lack of access to nonverbal cues. There is also less of a margin for error, given that the sessions are short and it is more difficult to reconnect with a client over the telephone if a rupture to the therapeutic alliance occurs. Attention to the factors described in this chapter will facilitate the successful delivery of telephone continuing care.

Maintain a Consistent Structure for the Calls

As much as possible, phone call appointments should be at the same time each week. The clinician's consistency and availability at that time set an important tone and will serve to communicate to the client the importance of the phone sessions. Also, a consistent structure during the call helps the client anticipate the clinician's questions regarding recent status, upcoming high-risk situations, and goals, rather than have to rely on hearing everything perfectly.

Each telephone contact should start with the structured Progress Assessment of current risks and protective factors. In one of our current cocaine continuing care studies, for example, we assess three general factors (recent alcohol or drug use, HIV risk behavior, and attendance at any current face-to-face treatment); five "risk" factors (compliance with medical or psychiatric treatment, depression, low self-efficacy, craving, and being in high-risk situations); and five "protective" factors (coping efforts in high-risk situations, sober social/leisure activities, pursuit of personal goals, self-help meeting attendance, and contact with a sponsor). Data gathered in this brief assessment are used to monitor current status, note changes in symptoms and functioning over time, select issues to focus on in the rest of the session, guide decisions about possible changes in level of care, and trigger case management efforts. This assessment brings considerable structure to the telephone sessions and helps to keep them from turning into "chat" sessions.

The longer the clinician and the client work together using the telephone protocol, the more the session will take on a conversational tone, but initially the phone sessions may feel awkward due to their newness, their brevity, and the structure of the protocol. To keep the telephone sessions sounding fresh and spontaneous, as opposed to overly scripted, it is best if clinicians develop their own approach to covering the required material. What we provide are sample scripts that might be useful in developing such an approach.

Pay Careful Attention

Counselors should keep the conversation somewhat faster paced, with none of the extended silences that might be appropriate when meeting in person. The clinician also must listen more carefully simply to understand the client's words. The sound is somewhat degraded at best, and it is common to hear other conversations or a TV playing in the background. The lack of nonverbal communication means that the clinician must pay close attention to the client's manner on the phone in order to guess at aspects of the client's demeanor that would be immediately obvious in person. The clinician must make these additional efforts at paying attention in a setting where, because of the lack of face-to-face contact, it may be tempting to try to read e-mail, take care of routine paperwork, or otherwise multitask. We encourage clinicians to resist these temptations and give the calls the same status and degree of focused attention that they would give an in-person session. Clients notice when the clinician is preoccupied while on the telephone, and they feel less connected and understood in response.

Clinicians must also be careful to note any signs of trouble in what is either said or not said by the client, and they should address these issues rather than ignore them. Although sessions with clients who are doing well may at times be quick "check-ins," if sessions are routinely empty and boring, this is a good sign that important issues are being avoided!

Be Warmer and More Effusive in Your Affirmation of the Client

Enthusiastic expressions of appreciation for the client's successes that might sound phony or over-the-top in person often sound just about right on the phone. It is very important to give the client plenty of positive comments about her commitment to treatment, in addition to calling on time, having the Client Workbook available, filling out the Progress Assessment form prior to the session, and so forth.

Encourage a Recovery Support Structure

In addition to consistency of telephone appointments, it is desirable for clients to establish additional social supports for recovery early in treatment. These may include the following:

- regular attendance at AA, NA, or other types of support groups and the ability to talk with another sober person before, during, or after the meetings
- connection with a sponsor and willingness and awareness of how to utilize the sponsor in recovery
- some other established way for the client to experience meaningful social contact, such as church participation, work, family contact, school or a training program, or involvement with a pet

In many cases, however, establishing these social supports becomes a longer-term goal of continuing care. Regardless of the strength of the client's support system, the clinician's awareness of the establishment and utilization of these structures throughout continuing care will make it easier to listen for the development of any cracks in the structure(s), which should be interpreted as potential "red flags."

Address Red Flags and Act on Concerns

Clinicians should listen for changes in behavior patterns that might indicate cause for concern, particularly things the client has identified as "red flags." Some clinicians are initially uncomfortable working with a client whom they cannot directly observe or get urine samples from to verify reports of abstinence. Our experience is that clients will admit to problems, including substance use, during telephone calls. However, there is surely some degree of underreporting, and at times outright misrepresentation, about episodes of substance use. In these cases, clients invariably end up conveying that they are in trouble, usually by missing scheduled telephone calls or sounding superficial or avoidant on calls they do make. An experienced addictions clinician will quickly figure out what is happening. As described later, we will often invite clients in for a face-to-face session—and ask for a urine sample—if we have reason to believe that they have started using alcohol or drugs again. The important point is that the maintenance of an alliance in a telephone-based continuing care intervention requires that the clinician act on concerns and not succumb to the temptation to let something go without addressing it.

Record Every Session

> Digital audio recorders are available for around $100, and recordings can be made by patching a cable into the telephone receiver line and plugging it directly into the audio recorder. These patching cables are less than $25, and no microphones are needed. This equipment can produce high-quality digital audio recordings that capture everything said by the clinician and the client.

Audio recording of treatment sessions can be very helpful in learning to deliver telephone continuing care protocol. The recordings can be used in several ways. You can listen to your sessions to determine whether all the elements of the program were successfully addressed. We have included a rating form on the CD-ROM (see the Telephone Adaptive Continuing Care Treatment Adherence Checklist), which can be photocopied and used for this purpose.

Peers or supervisors can also listen to and rate the tapes for adherence to the protocol, using the same form. In addition, being able to revisit sessions is particularly helpful as you are learning the protocol. To get over any initial self-consciousness about being recorded, we recommend you consider initially recording every session. Over time, awareness of the recording process will drop for you and for your clients, and more intermittent or targeted taping is usually sufficient.

Chapter 4

The Orientation Session

THE ORIENTATION SESSION IS INTENDED TO HELP you and the client develop rapport, provide the client with the information he needs about the program, identify targets for ongoing monitoring, and shore up motivation for recovery and commitment to treatment.

Before the orientation session, review the client's progress to date and be prepared to share what you consider to be relevant relapse risks and recovery goals. If you have not yet met the client, review available information regarding his addiction and recovery history, co-occurring problems, and treatment progress to date.

During the session, even though you need to convey quite a bit of information about the structure and content of the program, the tone of the session should remain collaborative. As you discuss procedures and treatment goals, be alert to issues that may pose a problem with treatment engagement or lead to early dropout. For example, clients who live in halfway houses, recovery houses, or transitional housing may have limited access to a phone; clients without a land line may not have enough minutes on their cell phone. Clients whose lives are chaotic in the wake of their active addiction, or who are coping with co-occurring problems, may have difficulty calling at the scheduled time. Clients who return to work or resume child care responsibilities may not view the calls as a priority. Clients may not think it's important to call if they are doing well; conversely, clients may not want to call if they are doing poorly or haven't followed through on their goals.

Finally, allow enough time at the end of the session to take care of any administrative matters. Here is a detailed outline of the orientation session:

STEP 1 ▸▸▸
Develop rapport and set the agenda for the orientation session.

1. **Welcome the client.** Acknowledge her progress and congratulate her for her achievement so far. Demonstrate appreciation for her commitment to participating in continuing care.

2. **Elicit questions or comments** regarding the procedures (such as additional paperwork), if any, that she may already have completed before your session, and respond appropriately. Let the client know how long the session will last and what it will include.

STEP 2 ▸▸▸
Explain the telephone-based continuing care program.

1. **Review the basic procedures briefly.** Tell the client that there will be regular phone calls in which you will touch base about how he is doing, provide some feedback about what you are hearing, and work with him to overcome relapse risks and achieve his goals. Explain that the exercises on the client worksheets will help him throughout the program.

2. **Engage the client in some discussion** about how he may find the calls helpful, and begin to troubleshoot barriers to participation. You may, for example, ask the client:

   What about this sounds most helpful to you?

   What might get in the way of completing phone calls?

3. **Reinforce the importance of the phone calls,** being prepared for the phone calls, and being willing to ask for help. Remind the client to fill in the date of the next phone call on each Progress Assessment worksheet.

4. **Review any program-specific rules** regarding call completion, for example, your working hours and availability for rescheduling calls, whether the client may be discharged for failing to complete a minimum number of calls, and so forth.

5. **Discuss potential barriers to treatment.** As you get a sense of the client's current situation, note any issues that may pose a problem with treatment engagement or early dropout. Engage the client in problem solving, and ask him what he thinks you should do if he misses a call. For example, you may say:

   > **It sounds like your top priority is keeping your job, and you don't always know your schedule in advance. What do you think will be the best way to make sure we talk regularly?**

   > **You deserve a lot of credit for the work you've done up until now. Sometimes, when people are doing well, they don't think they need to continue with the calls. What do you think?**

6. **Discuss step-up care.** Explain to the client why increases in the level of care may be recommended at some point and how the telephone sessions will be used to make that decision. Explain that you and the client can adjust his treatment goals as he progresses and that you may recommend step-up care if he runs into difficulty. The details of this explanation will depend on the length of the continuing care program and available adaptive care options. At the very least, you should let the client know that you may recommend a higher level of care if he relapses or if the Progress Assessment indicates that he needs additional support. Tell him, for example:

   > **We're going to set some treatment goals today, but we'll review them from time to time to make sure we are still working on things that are most relevant to you. If you keep on doing well, we'll stick with biweekly calls. If your risk for relapse increases, we might want to talk more often to help you get through whatever is going on at that time. If it looks like you need more support than I can offer on the phone, I may recommend that you come back to group for a while.**

   Stress that a recommendation for increased level of care is not a punishment. Rather, you and the client are working together to improve the client's substance abuse status, and if the current approach to treatment is not working as well as it should, another approach needs to be tried. You might say something like this:

> **If you went to your doctor because of an infection and the first medication she gave you didn't seem to be doing the job, you would want your doctor to either increase the amount of the medication, add another medication to the one you were taking, or switch medications entirely. You would expect the doctor to keep adjusting your treatment until you got better.**

Obviously, treatment for substance abuse is different from that for infections in many ways, not the least of which is that stepped-up treatment usually requires a lot more work than switching medications. However, you may be able to increase the willingness of the client to go along with changes in the treatment protocol if you emphasize the message that "we're in this together, and let's see if making these changes will help you achieve your goals more quickly."

STEP 3 ▸▸▸
Identify treatment goals and targets for ongoing monitoring.

1. **Introduce the Client Workbook (on the CD-ROM).** Use the Staying Motivated exercise on page 3 of the workbook to begin a brief discussion of the client's progress so far. Frame the discussion in terms of helping the client to be even more proactive in managing her addiction—continuing to do what has been successful and catching problems in the early stages before they lead to relapse.

> **NOTE**
>
> Listen carefully, and guide the client to choose the most relevant items for ongoing monitoring. Don't push too hard in the initial session, especially if you don't already have a working relationship with the client, but ask permission to challenge her if needed as you go along. By the end of orientation, you should be able to specify high-risk situations, pro-recovery activities, and initial goals clearly enough to be able to ask about them in the Progress Assessment.

To open the discussion of progress, you may ask, for example:

> **How have things been going since you started treatment?**
>
> *[If the client has been abstinent in the past]* **What is different about this time?**
>
> **What are the most important things you are doing to stay alcohol and drug free now?**

To help shore up motivation and identify motivational "hooks" for later counseling sessions, you may ask:

> **What are your most important reasons for staying drug free now?**
>
> **What are the best things about recovery for you?**
>
> **What led you to seek treatment at this time?**
>
> **What gives you the most hope at this time?**
>
> **What are the "red flags" I should look out for that will let me know you are on the road to relapse? If I see that any of these things are happening, can I bring it up in the session?**

2. **Identify high-risk situations.** Use the workbook exercise Identifying High-Risk Situations on page 4 (on the CD-ROM) to help the client identify up to five high-risk situations for ongoing monitoring. Include external (environmental) triggers as well as internal (cognitive or emotional) triggers. Review past relapse episodes to help identify relapse risks. Discuss particular times of year—holidays, birthdays, personally meaningful anniversary dates—as possible triggers for periodic follow-up as well.

    Environmental triggers should be personally relevant situations that the client is fairly likely to encounter in the upcoming weeks or months. Common environmental triggers include certain times of day (such as "happy hour"), handling money, being in certain neighborhoods, stress at work, watching sports on TV, being around friends or family members who are using drugs or drinking, hooking up at a bar or party, or visiting a prostitute.

Cognitive and emotional triggers are distinct from the actual urge, desire, or craving for substances. You can use the commonly cited acronym HALT (hungry, angry, lonely, and tired) as a jumping-off point. Other common emotional triggers include boredom, frustration, depression, symptoms associated with psychiatric diagnoses such as PTSD, a weariness of struggling with recovery, or a desire for excitement or escape. It may be difficult for some clients early in recovery to identify the thoughts and feelings that lead to urges. In that case, continue to probe for thoughts and feelings associated with risky situations the client encounters over the course of continuing care, in order to help identify the ones most associated with urges to use substances.

Difficult interpersonal interactions (for example, conflict with significant others) that give rise to unpleasant emotions can be considered either situational or cognitive/emotional triggers. Categorizing the triggers is less important than remembering to include both internal and external cues for drug use.

For example, ask the client:

[If client has had no substantial abstinent time] **What have been the main barriers preventing you from staying alcohol and drug free in the past?**

What are the people, places, and things you know you need to stay away from in order to stay alcohol and drug free?

Are there particular dates, or times of the year, when you will need more support to stay alcohol and drug free?

What have been the most difficult parts of recovery for you?

3. **Identify pro-recovery lifestyle activities.** Use the workbook exercise Moving Toward a Rewarding Substance-Free Life on page 7 (on the CD-ROM) to help the client identify up to five pro-recovery social/leisure lifestyle activities for ongoing monitoring. The rationale is that simply "not using" is a starting point, but overall life balance is important for building and strengthening recovery in the longer term.

Many clients will relate to having relapsed when bored or socially isolated. Therefore, these should be activities that can promote development of an alcohol- and drug-free social network. For example, a client who enjoys reading may be encouraged to attend a book club, attend an author reading at the library, or take a creative writing class. Attendance at religious services or church events, if the client wishes, may be monitored in this category.

Clients who are overwhelmed by responsibilities at work or home may need to be reminded that having lunch with a co-worker, sitting with another mom while the kids play at the park, or even watching TV with sober family members can contribute to a balanced pro-recovery lifestyle. It may be difficult for clients who live in recovery houses or other supervised housing to identify relevant activities because they are subject to so much structure. If that is the case, identify one or two activities, if possible, and revisit them as the client begins to have more freedom.

Ask the client:

[If client has been abstinent in the past] **When you have been in recovery in the past, how have you spent your free time?**

Before you got involved with alcohol and drugs, what kinds of interests or hobbies did you have?

Whom do you interact with in an alcohol- and drug-free environment? What kinds of things do you do together?

4. **Identify goals.** Use the workbook exercise Setting Personal Goals on page 9 (on the CD-ROM) to help the client identify short-term and/or long-term personal goals for ongoing monitoring. There is room for almost limitless flexibility in setting specific goals. We generally encourage clients to consider long-term, "big picture" goals while also recognizing that many clients are not ready to think beyond remaining sober on a day-to-day basis. Individual programs may emphasize certain goals, such as achieving and maintaining employment or improving parenting skills.

If the client can identify one or more long-term goals, help her to set shorter-term goals that she can pursue during the interval between phone calls. For example, a client who wants to change careers may set as her first goal filling out applications to nursing school; a client who has been neglecting her chronic medical condition while in her active addiction may set as her first goal making an appointment to see the doctor. If the client is not ready to think in terms of goals beyond immediate sobriety, encourage her to elaborate on the activities she needs to do in order to strengthen her recovery, and revisit the topic of broader goals later. At a very minimum, the client should be able to identify a simple goal related to remaining substance-free in the interval between orientation and the first phone call.

Ask the client:

What are some of the personal goals you would like to achieve in recovery?

What will successful recovery look like to you?

What are the most important things you need to do right now to stay abstinent?

[If client has been abstinent in the past] **What was most helpful/important to you in staying abstinent in the past? What do you need to do differently in order to succeed this time?**

What might be a first step toward achieving this goal? What could you accomplish by the time we talk on the phone?

STEP 4 ▸▸▸
Introduce the Progress Assessment worksheet.

1. **Review the structure of the phone calls**—that you will begin with a brief assessment to see how the client is doing, followed by counseling and setting goals.

2. **Give the client a copy of the Progress Assessment worksheet (on the CD-ROM).** Go through it exactly as if you were on the phone. Ask the questions with a time frame of "in the past week." Take time to prompt for the specific risky situations, pro-recovery lifestyle activities, and personal goals you just identified. For example:

> In the past week, how often were you in the situations you identified as your people, places, and things? That means the risky situations that you checked off in your workbook. Let's take a look—yours were arguing with your wife, being around your brother, and being bored or angry. How often did any of those things happen in the past week?

3. **Elicit the client's thoughts and feelings about completing the measure.** Address any misunderstandings or misgivings the client may have about ongoing monitoring, and emphasize that accurate, honest responding is the most important aspect of the work.

4. **Provide feedback.** Show the client the Progress Assessment Scoring Guidelines, and review her Risk Factors and Protective Factors scores. Ask the client what she thinks about the feedback, and answer any questions she may have about the procedure. Remind her that you and she will keep track of her Risk Factors and Protective Factors scores from week to week as an early warning system to guard against relapse and also to help the client give herself credit for continued progress.

> As you can see, you can get up to two points for each item. Usually, if you are on the right track, your risk scores will be low and your protective scores will be high. You can keep track of the scores on your worksheet if you want, and I'll always let you know your scores for each call. The purpose of these scores is to be able to keep track of your progress and notice any small changes in the wrong direction before they turn into big problems.

STEP 5 ▶▶▶
Prepare the client for the interval before the first call.

1. **Ask about upcoming high-risk situations.** As in each call, ask the client what risky situations he is likely to encounter in the interval before the first phone call. Early on in the process, clients may need help identifying upcoming high-risk situations. Probe for the people, places, and things

identified for ongoing monitoring in addition to other common risks. Guide the client in briefly planning how he will handle any expected high-risk situations. As much as possible, elicit the plan from the client before adding your own suggestions.

> **What high-risk situations do you think you will face between now and when we talk on the phone next week? How about any of the people, places, and things on your list? And what about the football game on Sunday? Where are you going to watch that? What do you think is your safest choice?**

2. **Set a goal for the interval before the first phone call.** Help the client identify one or more specific goals to work on before the first phone call. The first phone call will be in just a few days, so this will be an opportunity to practice identifying very specific short-term behavioral goals or determine how to recognize progress toward longer-term goals.

3. **Take care of any outstanding administrative matters, and schedule the first phone call.** Depending on the structure of the continuing care program, you may have any number of administrative details to attend to before the client leaves, ranging from collecting co-pays to validating parking passes. Administrative matters relevant to the clinical success of telephone continuing care include obtaining or updating contact information and developing a crisis plan.

Get an emergency contact number. Because you will be working at a distance, it is essential to have complete and up-to-date contact information for the client. Obtain at least one emergency contact—someone whom you can call and with whom you can leave a message if you can't reach the client. If the client lives in an unstable or temporary living arrangement, the emergency contact should not be an apartment- or housemate, but rather a sober friend or family member with a stable address and working telephone.

Give the client the Emergency/Safety Contract. This contract is on the CD-ROM. It helps the client determine what to do and whom to call in case of a substance-related, medical, or psychiatric emergency. The telephone continuing care program may have round-the-clock crisis services available, but more likely the client will need to rely on other community resources in case of an emergency.

Schedule the first call. When scheduling the first phone session, anticipate the various logistical problems that often interfere with completing calls, such as scheduling conflicts and access to a phone. We have found that offering to provide sessions face to face can help engage clients who would otherwise not be able to participate.

Decide who makes the call. One important question to be addressed during the orientation session is who should be responsible for initiating the call—the client or clinician? There are pros and cons for each option. Asking the client to initiate the call communicates the clinician's confidence in the client's capacity to follow through with her commitment to the protocol and improve her life situation. It also sends a clear message that the client is responsible for her own recovery. Moreover, it allows the client to call in from wherever she happens to be at that point, rather than having to be at a designated place at the time of the call. Therefore, holding the client accountable for her role in the telephone contact should not be viewed as punitive, demeaning, or an infringement on her autonomy. On the other hand, busy clinicians may have difficulty accommodating late calls. In our experience, clients do not call when they are scheduled to at least 50 percent of the time, and in those cases, the clinician has to call in an attempt to locate the client and complete the scheduled session.

Therefore, we develop a call completion plan with the client during the orientation session. This process involves exploring the client's access to telephones, her preference for calling in or being called, contingency plans for times when initial attempts to complete a call fail, and so forth. The client is advised that she and her clinician will revisit this issue frequently during the protocol, in case modifications are necessary. The goal is to do whatever it takes to increase the likelihood of completed calls.

Chapter 5

The Telephone-Based Sessions

THE OVERARCHING GOAL OF THE INTERVENTION is to help clients manage their addiction proactively by (a) avoiding and/or improving coping with high-risk situations (people, places, and things) and emotional triggers for drug use and (b) developing a lifestyle rich with meaningful and rewarding activities unconnected or incompatible with substance use. Sessions are structured to include a review of the client's progress and an opportunity to troubleshoot the week(s) ahead.

This section makes reference to the adaptive care protocol we have used in our research. In it, the clinician makes adjustments to the content, intensity, and modality of treatment based on considerations raised in the Progress Assessment. *Content* refers to the topic areas covered in the call; to make the most of a fifteen- to thirty-minute encounter, it is essential to choose the most relevant content focus. *Intensity* refers to how often the sessions are held and how long the sessions are. Our protocol specifies that the frequency of treatment may be increased if indicated, and then decreased again as the client's situation and coping improve. In addition, session length may be increased in order to more fully process a problem or crisis. Finally, *modality of treatment* refers to whether contact is made over the phone or in person, and whether additional interventions are recommended in addition to, or in place of, continued monitoring and counseling.

The items on the Progress Assessment were selected based on prior research and clinical experience. They are divided into three sections: General Status, Risk Factors, and Protective Factors.

The first section assesses broad status considerations that will affect the overall conduct of the session. The remaining two sections of the Progress Assessment address the client's balance of relapse risk and pro-recovery lifestyle factors. Taken together, they will help guide the content of the session and assist the clinician in making recommendations regarding intensity and modality.

The first status item is substance use. If the client reports use of alcohol or drugs, find out when his most recent use was and obtain enough quantity/frequency information to make a clinical judgment about the content, modality, and intensity of treatment to be recommended. Be sure to show appreciation for the client's honesty and persistence.

- If the use appears to have been a "slip"—that is, a brief episode, with relatively low intensity of use and limited negative consequences, followed by a return to abstinence—then the *content* focus will include debriefing of the episode and review of the client's successful efforts to contain the slip before it became a full-blown relapse, all geared toward using the slip as a learning experience to guide further relapse prevention efforts. Anticipation of upcoming high-risk situations and recovery-oriented problem solving should be informed by the recent slip. Increased *intensity* of phone contact may be offered to provide the client with additional support in managing similar situations more proactively. In most instances, a slip will not affect the *modality* of treatment. However, the client may be encouraged to talk about the slip in self-help meetings or IOP.

- If the use appears to have been more extensive and/or intense, or if the client has not been able to return to stable abstinence, the *content* will again include debriefing of the initial relapse. More important, the focus will be on regaining abstinence. Both increased *intensity* of contact in the form of stepped-up phone calls and a change in *modality* in the form of an in-person evaluation session (and multisession relapse prevention protocol) should be offered. Furthermore, clients who have left IOP may be encouraged to reenter treatment.

- In the case of a severe relapse, the client may be encouraged to seek evaluation for detoxification or inpatient treatment to help him regain abstinence.
- Telephone monitoring and adaptive counseling is designed as an abstinence-oriented program, but not all clients will endorse a goal of complete abstinence from all substances. If a client continues limited substance use with no intention of stopping, session *content* will include efforts to encourage the client to reconsider how his substance use fits in with his recovery and overall personal goals. The general approach will be to "agree to disagree" with the client regarding treatment goals, while seeking permission to raise concerns about the client's substance use as they become apparent to the clinician.

In our current research, we have included additional status items assessing involvement in an IOP and any HIV risk behavior. The IOP status item is included because we have begun telephone continuing care as early as two weeks into treatment, with a goal of supporting treatment involvement. Therefore, it is essential for us to monitor during each call whether every client is still in treatment. The HIV risk item is included because one of the goals of our intervention is HIV risk reduction. Programs may substitute other relevant status items; for example, if a primary goal of a particular telephone continuing care program is to support employment, clinicians may ask about employment status at each contact and only address HIV risk if it is a stated goal of an individual client.

The second section of the Progress Assessment assesses items that are believed to be associated with greater risk of relapse. These include failure to follow through on medical and psychiatric self-care as indicated by attending scheduled appointments and taking medications, sustained depression, low self-efficacy for maintaining abstinence, thoughts and cravings to use, and exposure to high-risk situations or "people, places, and things" associated with drug use.

The third section of the Progress Assessment assesses personal strengths, resources, and pro-recovery lifestyle behaviors that are believed to be associated with sustained abstinence from alcohol and drug use. These include drawing on a repertoire of coping skills to manage high-risk situations and cravings, involvement in a sober social network, pursuit of personal goals that are incompatible with substance abuse, Twelve Step meeting attendance and involvement, and contact with a sponsor or other helper outside the substance abuse/mental health treatment system.

Rather than yielding a single score, the Progress Assessment provides the opportunity to explore the balance between risk factors and protective factors or "recovery capital" and to look at patterns over time. We recommend that clinicians consider stepping up treatment when the balance of Risk Factors and Protective Factors scores shifts four to five points in the "wrong" direction. As the client progresses in recovery, he may be encouraged to achieve a balance of recovery-oriented activities, such as meetings, and broader personal goal activities, such as building a sober social network and preparing to (re)enter the workforce.

Detailed Instructions and Sample Scripts

STEP 1 ▸▸▸
Acknowledge the client for the call and begin the assessment.

In order to cover everything in a brief call, you will need to move quickly to the Progress Assessment questions. Most clients respond favorably to the structure of the calls, and most clinicians find that an extensive check-in at the start of the call is not necessary once they get used to the Progress Assessment. Here is an example of how the call might begin:

> **Thanks for calling in on time. Are there any emergencies I should know about? Okay, let's get right into your worksheet. Do you have it with you now?** *[Listen for response.]* **Did you complete it prior to the call?**

Always acknowledge the client's participation with enthusiasm. If a client didn't call in on time or has missed one or more scheduled calls, reinforce her choice to resume calls and mention that you will address scheduling issues later. If the client doesn't have her materials on hand and can't obtain them quickly, continue with Progress Assessment prompts. At the end of the session, prompt her to locate her treatment materials before the next call, and offer to mail additional copies if necessary. But don't be overly concerned about it; clients vary in their usage of the workbook and printed forms. Some always follow along, and others never open the book.

If there is an emergency, ask the client to describe it briefly. In most cases, it will be enough to assure her that you will discuss it with her further after completing the Progress Assessment—as long as you really do follow through! If the client is very upset, it may be necessary to deal with the emergency situation before returning to the structure of the call. Even then, it may be possible to retain the "spirit" of the call by helping the client deal with the emergency without resorting to substance use.

STEP 2 ▶▶▶
Review the Progress Assessment items.

The Progress Assessment consists of three items on General Status (for example, substance use, HIV risk behaviors, and attendance at treatment), five Risk Factors, and five Protective Factors. The assessment begins with questions about substance use and medical issues:

> **How much of the time did you stay alcohol and drug free in the past week?**
>
> **In the past week, have you had any medical appointments? Any changes in prescribed medication? How often have you taken your medication as prescribed?**

Continue through the Progress Assessment items in order, recording the client's responses. Ask for clarification as needed, but avoid getting bogged down in a detailed discussion of every item. Be alert to how the client's responses bear on her stated goals since the last session and to longer-term treatment goals. Is she showing progress over time toward a pro-recovery lifestyle? Is she becoming more proactive in avoiding and managing relapse risk situations?

In longer-term continuing care, review the client's list of high-risk situations, emotional triggers, and recovery lifestyle items periodically (for example, every three months) to determine whether the items being monitored are still the most relevant and to identify new items for monitoring, if appropriate.

If the client is following along on her worksheet, let her know how each item is scored so that she may record it if she wishes. Continually affirm the client for sticking with the process and providing complete and accurate information, even when it's not all good news.

The Progress Assessment also provides guidance to clinicians on adaptive modifications and case management efforts linked to each item in the assessment. For example, adaptive treatment for clients who report depression involves providing relapse prevention (RP) focused specifically on coping with depressed mood as a potential relapse trigger and CBT-informed advice for mild depression. Case management for depressed mood involves referral and linkage to mental health treatment, if the client is not already receiving such care.

STEP 3 ▸▸▸
Provide feedback on Risk and Protective Factors.

Based on scoring of the Progress Assessment, give the client feedback on his progress. The feedback should address both what the scores for Risk and Protective Factors look like this week and how those scores may have changed from the last session. If possible, link scores to particular goals that the client may have had for the week. For example, the client may have had high craving scores at the last call, and as a goal for the upcoming week, he was going to practice some new ways of coping with cravings that were discussed on the call. If he did, in fact, practice the new coping behaviors and his craving score dropped, it is important to make that connection explicit:

> **Your total risk score is 3—you were in one high-risk situation and had a couple of urges to pick up. That's down from last time. Your protection score is 6, the same as last time. You used a lot of good coping skills to deal with the urges, and you've continued to attend meetings and work toward your goals. You still don't have much as far as sober activities. Does that sound right to you?**

It can also be helpful to clients if they can receive feedback on longer-term trends in their risk and protection scores, at least in certain circumstances.

> **Although your Risk Factors score is only a little higher this week than last, when I look back over the past couple of months, I see that the score has been climbing steadily for some time now. What do you make of that?**
>
> **We saw that your participation in self-help meetings is down a lot this week, compared to last week. I think this is important to note, because your level of participation over the past two**

> months has been really high each week. Maybe we'd better spend a little time on why you've abruptly cut way back on your meetings. Did anything happen?

If you notice anything of concern in the Progress Assessment, such as big increases in risk factors or decreases in protection factors, it may be important to focus on those issues when working on problem solving and coping responses later in the call.

STEP 4 ▸▸▸
Review progress/goals since last call.

By the time you complete the Progress Assessment, you may have a good sense of how things are going from the client's perspective. However, you may wish to get more elaboration before moving on. The purpose of engaging in a more detailed discussion of the past week is twofold: to reinforce successes and to begin to specify the nature of problems that may need to be solved. You may also be on the lookout for flagging motivation; don't assume that successful goal completion is equal to being satisfied with how things are going.

If a high-risk situation or treatment-related problem was anticipated and planned for, engage the client in a detailed description of how he implemented his plan. What did he feel good about? What was more difficult? If the client didn't complete his stated goal, what got in the way?

> You spoke up in a meeting for the first time! That's a big change for you. What was it like?

> How did it feel to tell your brother not to bring beer to your house anymore?

> You've been talking about taking the civil service exam for a while now, but it seems like it's been hard to follow through. What's getting in the way?

STEP 5 ▸▸▸
Identify upcoming high-risk situations.

Ask the client to think ahead to the interval between now and the next phone call. What situations might she encounter that could lead to cravings or increased risk for relapse? Probe for likely triggers and guide the client in considering how best to avoid relapse, if she does not spontaneously report a plan.

> When will you be around any of your people, places, and things in the upcoming week?
>
> You will be stepping down to a lower level of care at your treatment program. That's a great milestone, but sometimes people find it is harder to stay alcohol and drug free when they have less support. What do you think?
>
> May I share my concern about your plan? Most people in recovery find that watching sports at a bar isn't the best idea, even if they aren't planning on drinking. Can you think of anywhere else to watch the game?

The client may or may not identify any high-risk situations. Clients aren't required to identify something each time, but they should become better at anticipating potential risky situations and engaging in productive conversations about whether to avoid or cope with the situation. If a client who reports frequent triggers or cravings on the Progress Assessment has trouble anticipating high-risk situations, help her to see the connection between past difficult situations and the possibility that those same situations may arise in the foreseeable future.

> You've had thoughts of using after seeing your mother the past few weeks. Are you going to see her this week? Do you think that might be a risky situation? How do you plan to handle it?

Over the course of treatment, one of your goals is to help the client go from believing that relapse is something that "just happens" in an unpredictable manner to having a clear understanding of his own set of risky situations, what he needs to do to be on the lookout for those situations, and what coping behaviors are likely to be effective when he encounters these situations.

STEP 6 ▸▸▸
Choose the focus for the remainder of the call.

At this point in the call, you may have fifteen minutes or less for counseling before it is time to wrap up and schedule the next call. Use information from the Progress Assessment, the review of progress toward specific goals, and the information on potential upcoming high-risk situations in your discussion with the client on where to focus your problem-solving efforts. Also, you can invite the client to include any other pressing matters he may see as having more of a bearing on his ability to remain alcohol and drug free. If adherence to the call schedule is a problem, this is the time to get it on the agenda. Most calls should focus on the short- to intermediate-term future, informed by the lessons of the past. For example:

> **Your goals were to attend AA daily and talk with your doctor about problems you've been having with your Zoloft. You made it to AA, but you're still having trouble taking your meds. Bad moods are still a problem for you, and they may be a high-risk situation for you in the upcoming week. Which of these things should we focus on? Is there something even more important for your recovery right now?**

Setting the agenda may or may not be an explicitly stated process, but the content focus of the call should clearly be related to the client's current clinical status as indicated by the Progress Assessment. See the Progress Assessment Detailed Scoring Guidelines (on the CD-ROM) for suggestions for matching session focus to client responses. In most cases, it will be pretty clear what the focus should be for the rest of the call—generally it will be whatever issue seems to pose the most serious risk for relapse or what is bothering the client the most. It is usually more effective to select a topic that the client agrees is important. Clinicians will sometimes think an issue that the client is ignoring is in fact the most pressing problem, and they may feel tempted to try to persuade the client to focus on it. This can certainly be done in longer face-to-face counseling sessions, but it is very difficult in relatively brief telephone sessions. Therefore, it is best to select an issue that the client agrees is critical.

STEP 7 ▶▶▶
Engage the client in brief problem solving regarding target concern(s).

Once you have identified the focus of the call, engage the client in problem solving. In general, we don't teach problem-solving skills in routine calls, but rather model them as we guide the client through the steps of solving her particular problem. Encourage the client to generate a few solutions and select one for implementation. Provide information and advice as needed, but avoid telling the client what to do or getting into an unproductive exchange in which you offer helpful suggestions and the client rejects them. Avoid argumentation by responding reflectively to resistance and quickly getting back to the task at hand.

When solving the problem requires learning a new skill, such as anger management or assertive drink refusal, you will need to decide how much to attempt to accomplish over the phone and how much of the skill building needs to occur either in a focused face-to-face session or in another form of treatment altogether. In general, we encourage you to do some basic coaching on simple ways in which the client can use the new skill in a particular situation, but not to attempt comprehensive teaching of a complex skill in which the client is particularly lacking. For example, you may model, and have the client rehearse, appropriate ways to refuse drinks or ask others not to bring alcohol into her home. If the same client then identifies improving assertiveness as a goal, you may consider working on a week-to-week basis to identify and plan for situations calling for assertive responding. Or, you may determine that the client has such significant personal barriers to assertive responding that she needs much more extensive and focused work specifically in that area. In that case, you would most likely make a referral. If failure to respond assertively to a specific interpersonal stressor is leading to increased risk for relapse, you may consider step-up to a limited number of face-to-face sessions focused on reducing relapse risk.

When motivation is flagging, this may be a signal that the client is minimizing the negative consequences of substance use and the benefits of abstinence. Review the information gathered in the initial face-to-face session to help identify reasons for staying alcohol and drug free—what are the client's current thoughts on the topic? How can he best remind himself of the costs of use? Discuss the benefits of abstinence—and how the client can gain even more benefit from sober living. Consistent with motivational interviewing, avoid trying to persuade the client that abstinence will be more rewarding in the long run, but rather attempt to elicit the client's own personal motivation.

Most efforts in problem solving will focus on helping the client plan for upcoming high-risk situations. Some of the high-risk situations that our clients frequently encounter include the following:

- Serious problems with a spouse or romantic partner. These problems can be acute, chronic, or both.
- Major social events, such as parties, weddings, birthdays, and holidays, where alcohol and drugs are often available.

- Spending time with a romantic partner, important friend, or family member who is an active user.
- Neighborhoods with high drug use rates that the client either lives in or must pass through to get to work or school. The risk level goes up if the client also used to purchase alcohol or drugs in those neighborhoods.
- Presence of a co-occurring psychiatric disorder, such as depression or PTSD.

One crucial issue to consider is whether the client should avoid such a situation or attempt to more actively cope with it. To help determine this, it can be useful to ask three questions:

- **Can the risky situation realistically be avoided?** Some situations simply cannot be avoided, even when the client is vulnerable to relapse.
- **How stable is the client at this point?** Clients early in recovery and those who have recently relapsed may be better off avoiding the risky situation altogether. Conversely, those with more stable abstinence might be able to manage exposure to the risky situation, as long as they are armed with a coping plan.
- **Are there potential advantages to experiencing rather than avoiding the situation?** Theoretically, successful active coping leads to increases in self-efficacy, whereas avoidance coping does not. In addition, dealing successfully with a risky situation may lead to the elimination of that situation as a risk factor, which could remove a barrier to recovery.

There are many possible coping responses to risky situations. Research does not indicate whether any particular approach is better than another, although the relative effectiveness of responses may differ as a function of the three issues raised here and the client's preferences, skills, and recovery resources. Even the same client may find that different approaches are more or less successful in different situations or at different points in recovery. Some of the coping behaviors used by our clients include the following:

- avoiding the risky situation
- listing the benefits of staying abstinent and the costs—both immediate and longer term—of drinking or drug use
- bringing someone who does not drink or use drugs to the risky situation
- lining up a self-help meeting or some other supportive group or activity to go to right after the risky situation
- practicing what the client intends to do or say in the risky situation if offered a drink or drug
- developing a plan to exit the risky situation if craving begins or stress levels get too high

Because there is a limited amount of time on each telephone contact, it is important to select one or two possible coping behaviors or responses and practice them during the call. Just talking about the behaviors will not be as effective as actually practicing them. For example, in a discussion about refusing an offer of a drink, a client may say, "I'll say something like 'I'm not drinking tonight.'" While that may be helpful, it would be better for the clinician and client to role-play the situation, with the clinician playing the part of the person who offers the drink, and the client practicing an actual response. The clinician can up the ante somewhat by not taking no for an answer right away, and pushing the client harder to accept a drink.

There are also many opportunities for the clinician to help the client integrate his various structures and supports by shaping the client's goals in a way that models such integration: connecting his identified interpersonal relationship goals to people at church or meetings or work, for example:

Is that something you could discuss with your pastor?

What about asking your brother to go with you to _____?

When you meet with your sponsor this week, could you ask for feedback about this?

Program and community resources will vary, but in general, we remind clinicians not to try to provide comprehensive substance abuse, mental health, and social service care over the phone, but rather to make referrals as appropriate. Then, telephone contact can support the client in making the best use of those resources.

STEP 8 ▸▸▸
Set one or more goals for the interval before the next call.

The client should be reassured that she doesn't have to come up with lengthy or complicated tasks and goals. In fact, simple and brief is better, as long as specifics are provided. Help clients choose goals and tasks that are concrete and doable. It is better for the client to experience success at a modest goal than to fail at an ambitious one.

> **What do you intend to work on this week? What specifically will you do?**
>
> **Are you sure that going to a meeting every day is realistic for you? You have been getting to one each week. How about setting a goal of really going to two or three this week?**
>
> **Okay, you said you'll get to three NA meetings this week. The more specific you can be about it, the more likely you are to follow through, so let's see what we can figure out right now. You said you want to get one in before the weekend—can you get to one Friday after work? And which other meetings will you attend?**

STEP 9 ▸▸▸
Schedule the next phone call.

Schedule the next phone call. If compliance has been a problem, make sure the client agrees that the designated time will work for him. If necessary, engage in brief problem solving regarding compliance with phone calls, including having the Progress Assessment worksheet ready.

The Telephone-Based Sessions **53**

Chapter 6

Adaptive Algorithms for Stepped Care

THERE ARE SEVERAL POSSIBLE APPROACHES to devising an adaptive algorithm to adjust level of care on the basis of the client's progress or lack thereof. At one extreme, clinicians can be told to use their own clinical judgment and to recommend changes when they think it is advisable. Or clinicians can be given general guidelines for stepped care and be urged to make use of them as they see fit. We have tried to provide more formal algorithms to clinicians, which make use of data collected in the risk assessment at the beginning of each call.

Our simple and straightforward algorithm is keyed on changes in the balance between risk and protective scores, and also takes into account current status in IOP or OP treatment that the client may still be participating in:

1. If the client shows an increase in Risk Factors score and/or decrease in Protective Factors score that combine to an overall shift of four to five points in the "wrong" direction, the clinician should attempt to address it in a more comprehensive fashion during the call with the client. It would be appropriate to call and speak for longer than usual to address the recent change and help the client develop a plan to decrease risk-related behaviors and/or increase protective

behaviors. If the client can agree to a reasonable plan and is confident in her ability to remain abstinent, then the next call will be scheduled as usual.

2. If the client can't agree to a reasonable plan or is very concerned about using alcohol or drugs, or if the worrisome negative overall shift in Risk Factors/Protective Factors scores is maintained at the next call, then the clinician should do the following:

    a. Encourage the client to make use of treatment and commence "watchful waiting," if the client is still meaningfully engaged in IOP/OP.

    b. Increase frequency of contacts immediately, if the client is not engaged in IOP/OP.

3. The usual starting point for increased frequency of contacts would be a scheduled call at half the usual interval (for example, if the client has been calling every two weeks, offer a call at one week) with the availability of emergency calls sooner, if needed. If the client is not confident she can remain alcohol and drug free for that time period, then the clinician should decrease the interval by half again and consider a face-to-face session (see item 4 below). If the client can follow through on her plans, then the clinician can continue with increased call frequency until the risk/protection balance shifts back to a healthier ratio.

4. The clinician should offer a face-to-face evaluation session if the following occurs:

    a. The client expresses low confidence in her ability to remain abstinent for at least one week.

    b. The client has difficulty following through on plans to lower risk/increase protection with phone contact.

    c. The nature of the client's problem requires case management that is too cumbersome to do over the phone.

Further Therapeutic Options on the Stepped-Care Ladder

If a face-to-face evaluation session raises further alarm bells, or if the clinically significant shift in the balance of risk and protective factors does not reverse itself relatively quickly, our algorithm calls for the implementation of further face-to-face treatment. We offer individual CBT/RP sessions (one to two per week) for four to twelve weeks to clients in this situation. Or we will help the client reengage with a local community IOP or OP program, if the client prefers that. In cases when the client has been engaged in a considerable amount of heavy drinking over an extended period, the possible need for formal detoxification also should be considered. Options for face-to-face, clinic-based stepped care are discussed further below.

Lateral Adaptations and Case Management Referrals

In addition to "vertical" moves via stepped care, the protocol provides guidance on when to consider what might be called "lateral" moves. In these situations, the client stays at the same level and frequency of contact, but the content of the intervention is modified. For example, decreases in self-efficacy might be addressed by rehearsing coping responses during the call and suggesting further confidence-building exercises between calls. Similarly, increases in depressive symptoms could be addressed by using CBT techniques that challenge cognitions and attributions associated with depression. These procedures qualify as adaptive treatment, as long as "if/then" statements are used to link specific scores on assessment items or measures to specific modifications in treatment. Recommendations for lateral adaptations and case management efforts are illustrated in the items from the Progress Assessment.

Face-to-Face Evaluation Sessions

We recommend that a step up to face-to-face contact be provided when the client reports relapse or if the client's balance of Risk Factors and Protective Factors as measured by the Progress Assessment remains problematic even after increasing the frequency of phone contact. It may also be provided if the client reengages after at least a month of no contact with the clinician. In most cases, a single session is scheduled within a week after the phone call in which the client reports use or heightened relapse risk, and depending on the outcome of the first session, a second session may be scheduled about one week later.

Step-up to in-person sessions is intended to accomplish one of several goals. In some cases, the client seems to be struggling in response to a particularly difficult set of stresses or risky situations. In those cases, expanded problem-solving efforts are usually initiated in longer and/or more frequent phone calls, and step-up to face-to-face sessions may provide an extra measure of support. In other cases, the client may come into the office for a session devoted to more intensive case management than can be done over the phone. For example, the clinician may assist the client in a computer search for nearby mental health treatment facilities and allow the client to use his phone to call for an appointment. In either of these cases, the structure and content of the session remains similar to that of a telephone-based session.

In some cases, it is necessary to take a step back from the usual routine and review the course of treatment as a whole, shoring up motivation and commitment to a new set of goals. These sessions are referred to as evaluation sessions, and differ in style and content from the usual continuing care session.

By the time an in-person evaluation session is scheduled, you may have spent several phone calls "putting out fires" with a client who is experiencing one or more crises, or who is showing minimal compliance or flagging motivation. If the client has been participating in phone calls, yet continues to do poorly, it is possible that the focus of the sessions and between-session goals has strayed off target. Therefore, rather than continuing to do more of the same, the goal of the face-to-face evaluation session is to take a step back from the immediate situation and get a broader assessment of what is going on.

The evaluation session will include a detailed debriefing of any relapse episodes as well as a review of the client's ability to cope with high-risk situations for relapse. There will also be the opportunity to address the client's motivation and commitment to abstinence from alcohol and drug use.

In some cases, it will not be possible to conduct this session in a face-to-face format due to transportation problems, the client's parenting or job responsibilities, or some other reason(s). In these situations, the session could be done over the telephone. However, it is important to convey to the client that the session will be longer than the standard telephone sessions (more like one hour) and that the client will need to be in a quiet room where he will be able to focus and talk freely.

Detailed Outline of Face-to-Face Session

1. **Set the agenda.** Affirm the client for taking the step of coming in to address his current problems, and set the agenda for the session. Include time for discussion of immediate concerns, but unless the client is in crisis, spend most of the time on a bigger-picture review of treatment progress. If the client is experiencing a crisis or needs substantial case management, attend to those needs right away and consider rescheduling the evaluation session.

2. **Debrief recent substance use.** Review recent episodes of alcohol and/or drug use in terms of the functional analysis or behavior chain. Identify, for each episode, the environmental trigger and thoughts and feelings that preceded resumption of substance use; the client's coping efforts, if any, and substance use behavior; and the short- and longer-term consequences of use. Identify patterns that can inform a return to abstinence. If the client has had a severe relapse, and poor social support and/or withdrawal symptoms are a major factor in continued use, then referral to inpatient treatment may be in order.

3. **Assess motivation.** It may be clear early in the session that the client is highly motivated to return to abstinence but lacks skills and/or resources to do so. In that case, it makes sense to offer additional treatment or referral to respond to the skill and/or resource deficit. However, low motivation is also often a barrier to resuming abstinence or making progress toward reducing relapse risk. Clients may have mixed feelings about giving up substances or about making the extensive lifestyle changes associated with successful recovery. Therefore, the face-to-face evaluation session includes formal assessment of motivation.

   Usually, at this juncture, it is most worthwhile to ask about motivation to regain or maintain abstinence from substances. In some cases, it may also be relevant to ask about following through with specific actions, particularly when the client has not followed through on referral to community resources to address a stated need. We find a set of scaling questions described by Rollnick and colleagues (Rollnick, Miller, and Butler 2007) to be particularly helpful in initiating a brief evaluation of the client's motivation.

These questions involve asking the client about importance and confidence for change as follows.

4. **Show the Importance Ruler to the client.** Print a copy of the Importance Ruler (on the CD-ROM). Focus on only one behavior change at a time, as you ask the client,

   "Using this scale, how important is it to you right now to stay drug free [stop drinking alcohol, get treatment for depression, etc.]**?"**

   ▸ If the client gives a number, ask,

   "Why are you at [that number] **and not 0?"**

   ▸ If the client points to the scale, ask,

   "Why are you here [pointing where the client pointed] **and not here** [pointing to 0]**?"**

   Listen carefully and with interest to the client's response with an attitude of seeking to understand the client's existing level of motivation. Briefly reflect back what you hear and ask for elaboration of vague or general statements. When you think you understand the client, offer a summary and ask if you have it right. If the client adds more, reflect the new information. Then ask,

   "What would it take to move you from [the number the client chose] **up to** [a number two or three points higher] **in importance?"**

   Again, listen carefully and reflect what you hear. Ask for clarification or elaboration briefly, if needed, in order to understand, and then summarize.

5. **Show the Confidence Ruler to the client.** Print a copy of the Confidence Ruler (on the CD-ROM). Ask,

   "If you did decide to stay drug free/stop drinking alcohol/get treatment for depression/etc., then how confident are you right now that you will succeed?"

   ▸ If the client gives a number, ask,

   "Why are you at [that number] **and not 0?"**

- If the client points to the scale, ask,

  "Why are you here [pointing where the client pointed] **and not here** [pointing to 0]**?"**

  Listen carefully and with interest to the client's response with an attitude of seeking to understand the client's existing level of self-efficacy for making the desired change. You will hear some change talk, mostly including ability and commitment to change but possibly also more desire, reasons, and need for change. Briefly reflect back what you hear and ask for elaboration on vague or general statements. When you think you understand the client, offer a summary and ask if you have it right. If the client adds more, reflect the new information. Then ask,

  "What would it take to move you from [the number the client chose] **up to** [a number two or three points higher] **in confidence?"**

  Again, listen carefully and reflect what you hear. Ask for clarification or elaboration briefly, if needed, in order to understand, and then summarize.

6. **Choose the focus of the session, based on your assessment.** If importance is low, or if the client states high importance numbers but can't elaborate, then motivational barriers, more than logistical or skills deficits, may be preventing progress. Suggested strategies to address low motivation include the following:

   - Acknowledge the difficulty of following through on action plans when feeling low motivation.
   - Use the client's response to "What would it take to increase importance?" to find hooks for increasing motivation. Provide information and/or personal feedback if applicable.
   - Review the client's responses to motivation-related questions at the start of treatment. How does the client feel now about what he stated then as the costs of using and benefits of abstinence?

- Continue to use a motivational interviewing approach of gentle inquiry, reinforcing change talk, and rolling with resistance.
- Encourage the client to commit to action consistent with his readiness to change, even if the only action the client is willing to make is to continue meeting with you.

If the client states moderate to high importance—that is, motivation—for change, but reports low confidence in his ability to follow through, then more traditional CBT training and/or case management may help to overcome barriers. Don't attempt to do everything in a single session; the purpose of the face-to-face session is to determine the course of treatment, not solve all of the client's presenting problems.

- Explore past and present efforts at change. What has worked in the past? What is different now?
- Use the client's response to "What would it take to increase confidence?" to guide problem-solving efforts.
- Determine whether the client needs additional support through a temporary difficult situation or whether the client needs more structured help with developing basic relapse-prevention skills. In the first case, stepped-up intensity of contact, with the usual call structure, may be in order. In the second case, step-up to a four- to twelve-week relapse-prevention protocol may be recommended. In either case, telephone continuing care may be supplemented with increased Twelve Step meeting attendance and/or return to group treatment.

Use the adaptive protocol to determine the next course of action—for example, return to phone calling, schedule additional session or recommend a course of RP.

Face-to-Face Treatment Options When Stepped Care Is Needed

In our adaptive protocols, clients who require more intensive treatment than can be provided on the telephone generally receive individual CBT/RP sessions. However, it is also possible to step clients back up to standard outpatient or IOP groups, if that option is more readily available, or if the client would prefer that. We usually recommend one to two sessions per week for four to twelve weeks, depending on the severity of risk level and the client's progress to date in the protocol. If individual treatment is an option and is preferred by the client, the following approaches are recommended:

Cognitive-Behavioral Therapy/Relapse Prevention (CBT/RP)

A number of versions of CBT/RP have demonstrated efficacy and are readily available in manuals, including these three:

- *A Cognitive-Behavioral Approach: Treating Cocaine Addiction* (Carroll 1998)
- *Treating Alcohol Dependence: A Coping Skills Training Guide* (Monti et al. 1989)
- *Combined Behavioral Intervention Manual: A Clinical Research Guide for Therapists Treating People with Alcohol Abuse and Dependence* (Miller 2004)

These manuals all share the same basic set of CBT components and many of the same procedures and exercises, including these:

- functional analysis of the client's relapse episodes
- methods for coping with cravings
- increasing motivation and commitment to abstinence
- assertiveness and drink/drug refusal skills
- improving decision making
- dealing with biased and distorted thinking
- coping and problem solving

Individual Drug Counseling

Mercer and Woody (1999) developed a treatment manual that standardized the approach to counseling that is typically taken in community-based programs, for use in a NIDA-funded multisite cocaine treatment study. This approach, which was referred to as Individual Drug Counseling, combines didactic material; elements of AA and other self-help programs; monitoring of substance use, craving, relapse triggers, and other high-risk situations; other relapse-prevention elements; management of free time; and spirituality. In the treatment study for which this intervention was developed, clients who received the individual drug counseling intervention plus group counseling had better outcomes than those who received cognitive therapy plus group counseling, a psychoanalytically oriented therapy plus group counseling, or group counseling only (Crits-Christoph et al. 1999).

Social Support-Based Interventions

Twelve Step Facilitation (TSF) is an individual counseling approach that was designed to help clients engage more fully with Twelve Step–based self-help programs (Nowinski, Baker, and Carroll 1995). TSF takes the client through the first five steps of Twelve Step programs, which involve acceptance of the self as an addict, surrender to a higher power, and completion of a moral inventory. Other topics include an examination of family history of substance use, learning about situations that lead to substance use, and sober living. This intervention was developed for Project MATCH and was found to be at least as effective as CBT and motivational enhancement therapy (MET).

Network Support, developed by Litt and colleagues (Litt et al. 2007), is a treatment intervention designed to help clients change their social networks to become more supportive of abstinence. Because AA was the most readily available potential source of support for abstinence, the intervention made use of components from the *Twelve Step Facilitation Therapy Manual* (Nowinski, Baker, and Carroll 1995). Making new acquaintances and engaging in enjoyable social activities through AA or other social networks were stressed, rather than other AA components like a higher power and powerlessness. For those clients who are not interested in AA, the intervention focused on increasing other forms of social support for abstinence.

Network Support was evaluated in a research study in which clients were randomized to a case management comparison condition (CM), network support (NS), or network support plus incentives for abstinence (NS+ContM). Data from the one-year follow-up indicated that both network support conditions produced better alcohol-use outcomes than the case management intervention. Moreover, NS led to greater increases in AA attendance and behavioral and attitudinal support for abstinence. Interestingly, the incentives did not improve outcome over network support alone, and in some cases appeared to actually decrease the effectiveness of NS (Litt et al. 2007).

If none of these individual treatment approaches is a viable option, standard outpatient treatment or IOP—both of which rely on group counseling—can also be used for clients who are not doing well in the telephone program.

Documentation

The clinician should document all contacts with the client and all attempts to reach the client. The clinician is responsible for keeping comprehensive records on each call, including a progress note and data regarding client adherence to the phone-calling process. (Samples of Telephone Continuing Care Progress Notes are provided on the CD-ROM.) Clinicians should note whether step-up care is recommended and whether the client follows through with the recommendation. This information can also be collected during the Progress Assessment. Referrals to outside services should also be documented, along with information about whether the client followed up on the referral.

Chapter 7

Maximizing Adherence to Telephone Continuing Care

AS WAS DISCUSSED EARLIER, it is crucial for the clinician and client to arrive at a calling plan during the orientation, particularly with regard to who should call whom and when. When a call is missed (for example, when the client does not call in or the clinician calls and there is no answer), it is the clinician's responsibility to try to reach the client, determine the reason for the missed appointment, and reengage the client in regular phone session attendance. The clinician should make active efforts to reengage a missing client for up to a month after a missed session, including phone calls to the client, phone calls to support people, and letters to the client. After a month from the last contact, the client is considered inactive in treatment but may return at any point during the treatment window (this will, of course, vary, depending on staffing and other resources).

Additional phone calls at various times of day in an attempt to catch the client at home are strongly encouraged. The idea is to engage in active, caring efforts to contact a missing client that stop short of harassing a client who does not wish to be found or overburdening the client's significant others. The following is a suggested sequence of retention efforts:

Client Does Not Keep Telephone Appointment

If the client is supposed to call in and has not called within ten minutes of the scheduled time, the clinician should call the client. If the client can be reached directly, the phone session should be done at that time, if possible. The clinician should inquire about the missed call. If the client has a plausible explanation, the clinician can simply review that the calls are the client's responsibility (whether the client is making or receiving them) and emphasize the importance of keeping the next appointment.

Even compliant clients are going to miss sessions occasionally. Therefore, if the client sounds "normal" to the clinician on the telephone, participates appropriately in the session, and seems to be following through with what she needs to do, her explanation that "I got busy and forgot the call" is likely to be true. In a case like this, the missed call may not be cause for concern—as long as this is not one in a series of missed appointments.

If the clinician does not contact the client, a message should be left, if possible, asking for the client to call. If the client calls back within one business day and has a plausible explanation for the missed appointment, the phone session should be conducted at that time, if possible. The clinician should remind the client of how important it will be to keep the next phone session, and problem solving regarding compliance should be done, if necessary.

Client Does Not Respond to Clinician's Message

If the client has not called back within one business day of the clinician's first message, the clinician should call the client again and leave another message stressing the importance of the client calling back. If the client calls back within a week of the missed call with a plausible explanation for the missed appointment, the clinician should conduct the phone session at that time and review compliance issues. Reasons for not calling back right away should be addressed, and solutions to these barriers should be identified. This is particularly true when the problem is lack of access to a telephone. It is our experience that a significant proportion of clients who begin treatment with a cell phone will either no longer have an active cell phone within a month or so or will have a new cell phone number. It is better to anticipate these problems than to have to react to them after they have happened.

After a week, the clinician should call the client again and leave another message, if possible. If the client does not call back within one day, the clinician should call one of the client's support persons, if applicable. If the client calls back within another week (that is, two weeks after the missed appointment), the clinician should evaluate the current status to determine whether a face-to-face session is needed to get the continuing care protocol back on track. The evaluation should review the goals and importance of phone counseling, counseling agreements, and problem solving to maximize compliance. The clinician should evaluate whether co-occurring problems, such as psychiatric symptoms, child care issues, other problems with children, or basic needs, are contributing to poor compliance and provide referrals if needed.

Client Does Not Respond within Two Weeks of Missed Appointment

If there is no response by the two-week point, the clinician should send a letter requesting that the client call back as soon as possible. The letter should emphasize the clinician's concern for the client and that the client is welcome back to treatment regardless of what has been going on in the meantime. If the client calls back, the clinician should evaluate the client's current status according to the risk assessment to determine whether a face-to-face session is desired to get counseling back on track. As was discussed above, the clinician should review the goals and importance of phone counseling, counseling agreements, problem solving to maximize compliance, and co-occurring problems. The compliance issues may be seen as a "red flag" warranting an increased level of care or an in-person evaluation session before returning to the regular phone schedule.

Client Does Not Respond within Four Weeks of Missed Appointment

The clinician should call the client again (and the support person, if applicable). If there is no response, a second letter should be sent letting the client know that the clinician will no longer actively seek him out at this time, but that he is still eligible to participate in treatment if he decides to do so at a later date. (In our studies, this "open door" is extended for up to twenty-four months.)

Client "Disappears" and Then "Reappears"

The clinician should talk with the client on the telephone about the client's absence and nonresponse to phone messages and letters. The clinician then should set up a brief (thirty- to forty-five-minute) face-to-face meeting with the client to review goals, agreements, and so forth, and also to take a urine drug screen (UDS) and breath test. If the client denies use of drugs/alcohol but complies with biological tests, the time of the next telephone appointment is reviewed with emphasis on the importance of keeping the appointment.

Enlisting the Contact Person

People nominated by the client as a contact person can be quite helpful in locating the client when she has stopped making telephone calls. Clinicians should always thank these people for their help! Repeated calls searching for the client may be annoying or intrusive to the contact person. When trying to reach a client who has missed an appointment, clinicians should ask the contact person's permission to call him or her again after a certain interval has elapsed and the client has not called.

Addressing Problems with Compliance versus Problems with Substance Use

It can sometimes be helpful to consider different modifications to treatment, depending on whether the client is having problems with substance use, compliance, or both. In that regard, there are four possible categories that clients will fall into when they participate in continuing care:

- The client is doing well with regard to substance use and is exhibiting good compliance with treatment.
- The client is doing well with regard to substance use but is beginning to have compliance problems with one or more aspects of the protocol.
- The client is using alcohol or drugs but is still exhibiting good compliance with treatment.
- The client is using alcohol or drugs and is having compliance problems with treatment.

Here are basic outlines for how each of these situations should be dealt with in telephone sessions.

Doing Well with Good Compliance

In this situation, stepped-up care is usually not needed, and the status quo can be maintained. In fact, when clients maintain this status for an extended period, it might make sense to talk about decreasing the level of care somewhat. It is crucial that the clinicians do the following:

- Demonstrate a continued high degree of interest in how the client is doing.
- Provide much positive reinforcement for a job well done.

Doing Well but with Slipping Compliance

Clients in this position fall into two groups: those who are really doing well and are feeling they need less treatment, and those who are heading for trouble. The clinician should be able to determine which group such a client fits into by taking stock of his current status in a number of areas and listening carefully to his explanations for not attending treatment sessions as consistently as before.

For example, a client who is actively involved in self-help, has a sponsor, and talks excitedly about how well work is going is likely in the "really doing well" group. Conversely, a client who is not strongly connected to a pro-recovery organization, or who reports feeling bored, lonely, or underappreciated at work, is more cause for concern when compliance is also slipping.

For clients in the "really doing well" group, the clinician should provide considerable positive feedback but also inquire about reasons for lack of compliance. If the explanation given makes sense— "I'm going to AA meetings four nights a week, and it's just hard for me to get to my counseling sessions at the clinic or make this telephone call since I want to spend some evenings with my kids"— further discussion about how to adjust treatment is warranted. In such a case, the clinician might say:

> **What you are telling me sounds reasonable. Perhaps we should change your treatment plan to cut back on outpatient sessions, but stay with the weekly telephone calls. As long as your compliance with this new plan is good, we can stay**

at that level—unless we decide together that you need more support, or you start to miss sessions or telephone calls.

For clients in the "cause for concern" group, the clinician should once again provide positive feedback but should directly bring up the behaviors that are worrisome. For example:

> **Over and over, we've seen that when clients are not feeling excited about and satisfied with their life during recovery, they are vulnerable to relapse. You've told me that you're lonely and feeling depressed, and the job that you were feeling really good about at first is turning out to be a real disappointment. So, even though you're maintaining abstinence and still going to work, I'm worried that you're headed for trouble. More evidence of that is that you have begun missing some of our telephone calls, and your attendance at AA has clearly slipped. What do you think about all this?** *[Listen to response.]* **Do you have any concerns about possible relapse?** *[Listen to response.]* **Do you think you should be making any changes now to your recovery plan?**

Having Problems but with Good Compliance

These clients are likely to respond favorably to changes in treatment given that they are already compliant. Still, it is important for the clinician to carefully discuss her rationale for wanting to change the client's treatment in some way—most likely by adding additional telephone calls, or possibly face-to-face counseling sessions:

> **You've really been very consistent about making your telephone calls. And it looks like your relationship with your husband has improved. However, you've also told me that you've started drinking on the weekends, and last weekend you got pretty drunk and it scared you. How does weekend drinking fit with the goal of abstinence that you expressed when you started treatment?** *[Listen to response.]* **It sounds like you now believe that it is safe to drink on the weekends if you can keep it under control. What about your prior attempts to drink or use drugs in a controlled fashion?** *[Listen to response.]* **How did those work out?** *[Listen to response.]* **Why should it be any different this time?**

At this point, you should hope that the client will come to the conclusion that any substance use is dangerous and that she needs to take action to get back to stable abstinence. It is best if she can come up with new goals regarding her behavior. However, if she is having trouble with this and is open to recommendations, the case clinician can make suggestions.

> **If it is okay with you, I can offer a few suggestions. For example, it sounds like we need to make some changes to your treatment, to make sure that the drinking stops now before it gets worse. I think that it might be time for you to start attending relapse-prevention sessions here at the clinic. What do you think?**

The specific changes to recommend with a compliant client will depend on the nature of the problem—how severe the substance abuse or co-occurring problems have become, and so forth—and the client's life circumstances and preferences. With compliant clients, one can be tempted to "pile on" additional treatment, since they are not as likely to outright refuse to attend. However, too much additional treatment can turn a compliant client into a resistant one, so the costs and benefits of more treatment should be considered carefully. Approaching the situation as a problem that the clinician and the client need to address together may increase the chance that any changes that the two decide on will actually be made.

Having Problems and Poor Compliance

These clients are going to be the most difficult to manage in telephone continuing care. The fact that they are already having problems with compliance suggests that any additional treatment the clinician recommends will lead to more compliance problems. Here are the factors to consider before formulating a change in treatment:

- Evaluate how serious the substance use problem is at this point.
- Determine why the client isn't being compliant.
- Evaluate whether better compliance with the current level of care is likely to take care of the problem, or if an increase in frequency or intensity of treatment or a switch to an entirely different therapeutic approach is warranted.

- Evaluate whether co-occurring problems, such as psychiatric symptoms, relationship problems, child care issues, other problems with children, or basic needs, are contributing to the substance use problems or poor compliance.

If the clinician thinks that the main problem is poor compliance, her first task is to figure out a way to get the client back in treatment. It may make more sense to first attempt to get the client to attend the various sessions that were part of the treatment plan prior to compliance problems, rather than add additional sessions. However, the client may have had objections to certain aspects of that prior treatment plan, and so a substitution of some sort may be warranted. It is possible the client may even be willing to participate in treatment of greater intensity, if the clinician can assist her in removing whatever barriers are preventing better compliance. The important point is that the clinician should actively reach out to the client. Obviously, the more time that passes while the client is having problems and not being compliant with treatment, the less the chances are of achieving a good outcome.

Other problems will arise that have not resulted in relapse but pose a threat to continued sobriety. Such problems might include a change in health status, loss of job, loss of a relationship/significant person, or poor compliance with medications. These will potentially require increased clinician contact with the client and further case management with additional referrals. In situations such as these, procedures should be followed to help the client develop discrepancy between expressed goals and current behaviors. Moreover, the client should always be encouraged to state what she thinks she should do or what sort of support she would find helpful. If the plan developed by the client sounds good to the clinician, methods for implementing it can be discussed. If the plan does not seem adequate to the clinician, suggestions for changes should be made. These might include offering an option of accepting increased structure to help the client get through this "rocky time" with the least additional stress. Any of the above options might be offered, including a brief return to more intensive treatment (that is, IOP or residential) for stabilization or increased face-to-face contact with the clinician. The goal of the clinician in such situations is to help the client get through the crisis with as little damage as possible and to facilitate the client's connection to and utilization of established resources and structure.

References

American Society of Addiction Medicine. 2001. *ASAM PPC-2R-ASAM patient placement criteria for the treatment of substance-related disorders.* 2nd ed. Chevy Chase, MD: American Society of Addiction Medicine.

Amrhein, P. C., W. R. Miller, C. E. Yahne, M. Palmer, and L. Fulcher. 2003. Client commitment language during motivational interviewing predicts drug use outcomes. *Journal of Consulting and Clinical Psychology* 71:862–78.

Baer, L., M. W. Brown-Beasley, J. Sorce, and A. I. Henriques. 1993. Computer-assisted telephone administration of a structured interview for obsessive-compulsive disorder. *American Journal of Psychiatry* 150:1737–38.

Baer, L., D. G. Jacobs, P. Cukor, J. O'Laughlen, J. T. Coyle, and K. M. Magruder. 1995. Automated telephone screening survey for depression. *Journal of the American Medical Association* 273:1943–44.

Carroll, K. M. 1998. *A cognitive-behavioral approach: Treating cocaine addiction.* NIH publication 98-4308. Rockville, MD: National Institute on Drug Abuse.

Connors, G. J., A. R. Tarbox, and L. A. Faillace. 1992. Achieving and maintaining gains among problem drinkers: Process and outcome results. *Behavior Therapy* 23:449–74.

Crits-Christoph, P., L. Siqueland, J. Blaine, A. Frank, L. Luborsky, L. S. Onken, L. Muenz, M. E. Thase, R. D. Weiss, D. R. Gastfriend, G. Woody, J. P. Barber, S. F. Butler, D. Daley, S. Bishop, L. M. Najavits, J. Lis, D. Mercer, M. L. Griffin, K. Moras, and A. T. Beck. 1999. Psychosocial treatments for cocaine dependence: National Institute on Drug Abuse Collaborative Cocaine Treatment Study. *Archives of General Psychiatry* 56:493–502.

Dennis, M. L., and C. K. Scott. 2007. Managing addiction as a chronic condition. *Addiction Science and Clinical Practice* 4:45–55.

Dennis, M. L., C. K. Scott, and R. Funk. 2003. An experimental evaluation of recovery management checkups (RMC) for people with chronic substance use disorders. *Evaluation and Program Planning* 26:339–52.

Foote, A., and J. C. Erfurt. 1991. Effects of EAP follow-up on prevention of relapse among substance abuse clients. *Journal of Studies on Alcohol* 52:241–48.

Greist, J. H., I. M. Marks, L. Baer, J. R. Parkin, P. A. Manzo, J. M. Mantle, K. W. Wenzel, C. J. Spierings, K. A. Kobak, S. L. Dottl, T. M. Bailey, and L. Forman. 1998. Self-treatment for obsessive compulsive disorder using a manual and a computerized telephone interview: A U.S.–U.K. study. *M.D. Computing* 15:149–57.

Horng, F., and K. Chueh. 2004. Effectiveness of telephone follow-up and counseling in aftercare for alcoholism. *Journal of Nursing Research* 12:11–19.

Humphreys, K., and J. A. Tucker. 2002. Toward more responsive and effective intervention systems for alcohol-related problems. *Addiction* 97:126–32.

Institute of Medicine. 2006. *Improving the quality of health care for mental and substance-use conditions: Quality chasm series.* Washington, DC: National Academies Press.

Lavori, P. W., R. Dawson, and A. J. Rush. 2000. Flexible treatment strategies in chronic disease: Clinical and research implications. *Biological Psychiatry* 48:605–14.

Lichtenstein, E., R. E. Glasow, H. A. Lando, D. J. Ossip-Klein, and S. M. Boles. 1996. Telephone counseling for smoking cessation: Rationales and meta-analytic review of evidence. *Health Education Research* 11:243–57.

Litt, M. D., R. M. Kadden, E. Kabela-Cormier, and N. Petry. 2007. Changing network support for drinking: Initial findings from the network support project. *Journal of Consulting and Clinical Psychology* 75:542–55.

Lynch, K. G., D. Van Horn, M. Drapkin, M. Ivey, D. Coviello, and J. R. McKay. 2009. Moderators of response to extended telephone continuing care for alcoholism. Manuscript under review.

McKay, J. R. 2005. Is there a case for extended interventions for alcohol and drug use disorders? *Addiction* 100:1594–1610.

McKay, J. R. 2009a. *Adaptive continuing care and the management of substance use disorders.* Washington, DC: American Psychological Association Press.

McKay, J. R. 2009b. Continuing care research: What we've learned and where we're going. *Journal of Substance Abuse Treatment* 36:131–45.

McKay, J. R., K. G. Lynch, H. M. Pettinati, and D. S. Shepard. 2003. An examination of potential sex and race effects in a study of continuing care for alcohol- and cocaine-dependent patients. *Alcoholism: Clinical and Experimental Research* 27:1321–23.

McKay, J. R., K. G. Lynch, D. S. Shepard, J. Morgenstern, R. F. Forman, and H. M. Pettinati. 2005a. Do patient characteristics and initial progress in treatment moderate the effectiveness of telephone-based continuing care for substance use disorders? *Addiction* 100:216–26.

McKay, J. R., K. G. Lynch, D. S. Shepard, and H. M. Pettinati. 2005b. The effectiveness of telephone-based continuing care for alcohol and cocaine dependence: 24-month outcomes. *Archives of General Psychiatry* 62:199–207.

McKay, J. R., K. G. Lynch, D. S. Shepard, S. Ratichek, R. Morrison, J. Koppenhaver, and H. Pettinati. 2004. The effectiveness of telephone-based continuing care in the clinical management of alcohol and cocaine use disorders: 12-month outcomes. *Journal of Consulting and Clinical Psychology* 72:967–79.

McKay, J. R., K. G. Lynch, D. Van Horn, M. Ivey, D. W. Oslin, and M. Drapkin. 2009a. Effectiveness of extended telephone continuing care: 18-month outcomes. Presented at the Research Society on Alcoholism conference, San Diego, CA.

McKay, J. R., K. G. Lynch, D. Van Horn, K. Ward, and D. Oslin. 2008. Effectiveness of extended telephone continuing care. Presented at the annual Research Society on Alcoholism meeting, Washington, DC.

McKay, J. R., D. Van Horn, D. Oslin, K. G. Lynch, M. Ivey, K. Ward, M. Drapkin, and D. Coviello. 2009b. A randomized trial of extended telephone-based continuing care for alcohol dependence: Within treatment substance use outcomes. Manuscript under review.

McLellan, A. T., D. Carise, and H. D. Kleber. 2003. The national addiction treatment infrastructure: Can it support the public's demand for quality care? *Journal of Substance Abuse Treatment* 25:117–21.

McLellan, A. T., D. C. Lewis, C. P. O'Brien, and H. D. Kleber. 2000. Drug dependence, a chronic medical illness: Implications for treatment, insurance, and outcomes evaluation. *Journal of the American Medical Association* 284:1689–95.

Mensinger, J. L., K. G. Lynch, T. R. TenHave, and J. R. McKay. 2007. Mediators of telephone-based continuing care for alcohol and cocaine dependence. *Journal of Consulting and Clinical Psychology* 75:775–84.

Mercer, D. E., and G. E. Woody. 1999. *Individual drug counseling*. NIH publication 99-4380. Rockville, MD: National Institute on Drug Abuse.

Miller, W. R., ed. 2004. *Combined behavioral intervention manual: A clinical research guide for therapists treating people with alcohol abuse and dependence.*

Vol. 1 of COMBINE Monograph Series. NIH publication 04-5288. Bethesda, MD: National Institute on Alcohol Abuse and Alcoholism.

Miller, W. R., T. B. Moyers, D. Ernst, and P. Amrhein. 2003. *Manual for the Motivational Interviewing Skill Code (MISC)*. Version 2.0. Albuquerque, NM: Center on Alcoholism, Substance Abuse, and Addictions.

Miller, W. R., and S. Rollnick. 2002. *Motivational interviewing: Preparing people for change*. 2nd ed. New York: Guilford Press.

Monti, P. M., D. B. Abrams, R. M. Kadden, and N. L. Cooney. 1989. *Treating alcohol dependence: A coping skills training guide*. New York: Guilford Press.

Nowinski, J., S. Baker, and K. M. Carroll. 1995. *Twelve step facilitation therapy manual*. NIH publication 94-3722. Bethesda, MD: National Institute on Alcohol Abuse and Alcoholism.

Osgood-Hynes, D. J., J. H. Greist, I. M. Marks, L. Baer, S. W. Henerman, K. W. Wenzel, P. A. Manzo, J. R. Parkin, C. J. Spierings, S. L. Dottl, and H. M. Vitse. 1998. Self-administered psychotherapy for depression using a telephone-accessed computer system plus booklets: An open U.S.–U.K. study. *Journal of Clinical Psychiatry* 59:358–65.

Rollnick, S., P. Mason, and C. Butler. 1999. *Health behavior change: A guide for practitioners*. New York: Churchill Livingstone.

Rollnick, S., W. R. Miller, and C. C. Butler. 2007. *Motivational Interviewing in health care: Helping patients change behavior*. New York: Guilford Press.

Roter, D. L., J. A. Hall, R. Merisca, B. Nordstrom, D. Cretin, and B. Svarstad. 1998. Effectiveness of interventions to improve patient compliance: A meta-analysis. *Medical Care* 36:1138–61.

Simpson, D. D. 2004. A conceptual framework for drug treatment process and outcomes. *Journal of Substance Abuse Treatment* 27:99–121.

Sobell, M. B., and L. C. Sobell. 2000. Stepped care as a heuristic approach to the treatment of alcohol problems. *Journal of Consulting and Clinical Psychology* 68:573–79.

Wagner, E. H., B. T. Austin, C. Davis, M. Hindmarsh, J. Schaefer, and A. Bonomi. 2001. Improving chronic illness care: Translating evidence into action. *Health Affairs* 20:64–78.

Wasson, J., C. Gaudette, F. Whaley, A. Sauvigne, P. Baribeau, and H. G. Welch. 1992. Telephone care as a substitute for routine clinic follow-up. *Journal of the American Medical Association* 267:1788–93.

About the Authors

James R. McKay, Ph.D., is a professor of psychology in psychiatry at the University of Pennsylvania and the Director of the Penn Center on the Continuum of Care in the Addictions. He is also the Director of the Center of Excellence in Substance Abuse Treatment and Education at the Philadelphia Veterans Affairs Medical Center. Dr. McKay is the author or coauthor of more than 140 journal articles and book chapters. His work has focused on the evaluations of continuing care treatments for alcohol- and cocaine-use disorders, comparisons of outcomes following inpatient and outpatient rehabilitation treatments, the efficacy and cost-effectiveness of enhanced treatments for substance abuse, the impact of random assignment on outcomes, and the identification of factors over time that predict relapse following substance abuse treatment. His current work involves the development and evaluation of adaptive treatments for substance use disorders.

Deborah H. A. Van Horn, Ph.D., is an adjunct assistant professor of psychology in psychiatry at the University of Pennsylvania. She is also an independent consultant and trainer in counseling skills for lifestyle change. Her research has focused on evaluating new applications of cognitive-behavioral therapy and motivational interviewing in substance abuse treatment. Her training practice focuses on adapting empirically supported treatments for everyday clinical practice.

Rebecca Morrison, R.N., M.A., has worked in the field of addictions treatment and research for more than fifteen years. She has a master's degree in psychology with certification in addictions treatment and has worked in the department of psychiatry at the Penn Medical School. She is a registered nurse with certification in critical care and emergency nursing and is currently working in the medical intensive care unit of a large teaching hospital. She is pursuing graduate studies in bioethics.